Collaborative Computing

Multimedia Across the Network

Collaborative Computing

Multimedia Across the Network

Jeff Shapiro

AP PROFESSIONAL

Boston San Diego New York
London Sydney Tokyo Toronto

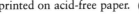
AP PROFESSIONAL
1300 Boylston Street, Chestnut Hill, MA 02167

An Imprint of ACADEMIC PRESS, INC.
A Division of HARCOURT BRACE & COMPANY

United Kingdom Edition published by
ACADEMIC PRESS LIMITED
24–28 Oval Road, London NW1 7DX

ISBN 0-12-638675-7

Printed in the United States of America
95 96 97 98   IP   9 8 7 6 5 4 3 2 1

This book is dedicated to my grandfather, Samuel S. Cohen, who taught me that "love of knowledge" relates to dissemination, not accumulation.

Contents

Preface

As much as we might like to think so, this book isn't about mere theory. It's about you, me, and the people that we work and interact with on a daily basis. It's about leveraging new technologies in new ways to do new things. And most of all, it's about keeping control of a rapidly changing situation in a rapidly changing world.

Collaborative computing is about multimedia. It's about networks. It's about how those two concepts collide and combine to form something new, different, and exciting. It will change how you view computers as tools, and it will offer tools that would have been considered impossible just a few years before.

You've seen the proliferation of nontextual information on computers. If you're an easy-going sort, you've implemented these technologies on individual machines on the network in a lassez-faire manner. If you're the type that believes in strong centralized control you kept this stuff off your network until user pressure forced you to consider making it available. Either way, it's decision time.

There are a number of issues to be addressed. On the technology side how are you going to provide these advanced features without having to completely throw away all of your current computing equipment? How are you going to go about bringing these new bells and whistles to the environment?

These questions are actually the easiest to answer. Any given technology almost always has a "best" way to implement. Getting from here (your current configuration) to there (your desired configuration) is simply a matter of planning and executing a series of mostly self-evident steps.

The management issues are thornier. How do we decide who gets which technology, and when? If we have x number of deserving people, but only y dollars, how do we decide who gets to play first?

That's the major focus of this book. Sure, we're going to talk about all the really neat computer things that you can add to your network to make it faster, friendlier, and a lot more colorful, but as we do that, we're going to talk about the real reasons for doing so, and what benefits can be expected to accrue from it.

The technologies described here are real, current, and available. Prices continue to be high, but as with all developing technologies that's not going to be the case for long. In the near future you will be confronted with the necessity of implementing one or more of the neat things discussed herein, and I hope this book will have helped to prepare you for that fateful moment. Good luck, and I'll see you on the Info Highway.

Jeff Shapiro
shapiroj@cerfnet.com
San Diego, California

About the Author

Jeff Shapiro is the manager of communications and information systems for Greenfield Environmental in Sand Diego, California. He manages a multimedia-enabled wide area network of 210 computers at eight sites in two states. In the past Jeff was a networking product manager, technical support manager, and reseller of networked accounting systems. He's also done time as a systems operator and programmer.

Jeff is an adjunct instructor (that means part-time teacher) in computer science/information systems at Grossmont College in El Cajon, California, where he teaches Introduction to Computers, Small Systems Analysis, and other courses. He writes a monthly column for *NetWare Solutions* magazine on management and technology issues, and occasionally contributes to *PC Novice* magazine. This is his first non-textbook.

Jeff was born in Montreal, but moved to San Diego at an early age, where he stuck. He attended San Diego State University, majoring in Information Systems and minoring in partying.

1

MULTIMEDIA ON THE NETWORK

The concept of networked multimedia is a <u>very</u> broad one. In this chapter we'll make some basic definitions and look at what life on a multimedia network can be like.

Do You See What I See?

Personal computers used to be such boring things. They were slow by today's standards and not very capable. If you wanted to store information, odds were that the information to be stored was textual—in the form of words in a document, numbers in a spreadsheet, or lists in a database.

Times changed. As small computers got more powerful they got more graphical, too. It became possible to store photographs, document images, sound, and even video either on the personal computer or on the network, and all it took was storage—a lot of storage. And power—a lot of power. More on both of these later.

What Is Multimedia, Anyway?

Multimedia breaks down into four components: document images, photographs, sound, and moving images. Each arrives in your computer a different way, is stored in a different format, and has to be managed uniquely.

Document Images

Document images are pretty simple. They can be images of an entire document that have been stored in the computer electronically, or graphics such as cartoons or business graphs. They can be brought into the computer in one of two ways: creation or importation.

The simplest way is to create them with the computer itself. Paintbrush programs, line-drawing programs, and purchased clip art are all methods of making and using computer-generated images. Once the images are in the computer they can be combined with other images or textual documents.

Images are stored in the computer as one of two types and in a wide variety of formats within those types. The first and most common type is called a *bitmap*, or *raster image*. Bitmaps take the image and reduce it to a series of individual dots called *pixels*.

If the image is a simple black-and-white one, each pixel is represented by a 0 if the spot is white and a 1 if the spot is black. Images that have greyscales (each pixel could be black, one of a number of shades of grey, or white) use more 1s and 0s for each pixel to store its current value. Color images have to store a lot of information, so up to 24 1s and 0s can be used for each individual pixel in the image.

Bitmaps are stored in any one of a number of common formats, including Personal Computer Exchange (PCX), Graphical Image Format (GIF), Windows Metafile (WMF), Device Independent Bitmap (DIB), Tagged Image File Format (TIFF), and Joint Photographics Expert Group (JPEG).

The other way to store images is to store the lines instead of the dots. This typically works only for line drawings like blueprints and such but it is a very efficient method for that sort of image. These images are called *vector images,* and the format they're stored in is usually specific to the program that created them, like AutoCAD or CorelDRAW!.

Bringing an existing image such as a photograph or document into the computer requires both specialized hardware and some specialized software. The most common way to get externally generated images into the computer is to use a scanner, which takes the document and reduces it to a bitmap of 1s and 0s that now represent the image digitally. If the image is of the right type, once it's in the computer you can convert it to a vector image by using a tracing program.

You can also use the common fax machine as a scanner if you have a fax board for your computer, but if you use this method the image's resolution will suffer. Resolution is an indicator of the stored document's overall quality and is measured in dots per inch. Fax machines typically scan documents at 200 dots per linear inch. Most scanners are capable of recognizing up to 600 dots per inch, so a scanned image will be much more accurate than a faxed one.

Photographs

Photographs usually make their way into the computer in the same way that document images do: by being scanned into a digital file. They are often scanned at a lower resolution than document images are because they are in color. The human eye considers color to be more important than detail, and a colorful image is more "pleasing" than a detailed one. Of course a colorful, detailed image is the most pleasing of all.

Color depth will also drastically affect the size of the file that your image is stored in. The lowest color depth is 16 colors, and you can store two pixels in a single byte of memory, but 16-color photographs are very poor quality. Photographic images will more commonly be stored in 256-color files, where each pixel requires a full byte of memory, or even in files that store 16.7 million colors per pixel, which requires three bytes (24 bits) of memory per pixel.

Black-and-white images are commonly stored in greyscale, which allows each pixel to be black, white, or usually up to 256 shades of grey. Each pixel requires one byte of storage.

Fax machines can also be used to import black-and-white photographs at low resolution. Color fax machines aren't in general use right now, but new technologies are being developed that may change that very soon.

These numbers sound huge, don't they? Six hundred dots per inch and a byte or more for each dot add up to some hefty files. Actually it's not nearly that bad. Once the image has been scanned (but before it is actually written into a file) it gets compressed. Because there may be hundreds or even thousands of adjacent pixels in an image that are identical, why store the same digital information over and over again? If the image has 1,000 identical pixels in a row, it will be stored as a "token" that says "compression time," the number 1,000, and the actual value for all those pixels. This usually reduces images to a small fraction of their "raw" size.

Sound

Sound originates from two possible sources: live or recorded. If it's live, it's usually captured from a microphone that turns it into a stream of digital information stored as a file on the computer, which can then repeat the information on request.

If the sound comes from a recorded source, it might be from an audio compact disc of your favorite band or a radio broadcast. We capture the stream of audible information and convert it to a file of 1s and 0s—the digital language of the computer. By using special data-capable musical instruments it can also be stored not as music but as instructions on how to play music. The instructions reside in a file that will be used to control instruments hooked directly to the computer to create the actual sounds.

Moving Images

Moving images are the newest category of multimedia. Computers just didn't have the power to capture, store, and display them until very recently. Applications include videoconferencing, which is live simultaneous transmission and reception of video (and sound) information, and recorded voice and video, usually on Compact Disc-Read-Only Memory (CD-ROM) because the files are very large.

These images can be stored in a number of formats, all of which are incompatible with each other. This can create problems (or opportunities depending on how you feel at the time).

Any individual computer can have none, one, some, or all of these components. If a personal computer has them all, it's called a "multimedia PC."

THE HOME/OFFICE PROBLEM

Today we see a huge disparity between the typical home computer and the typical office computer. Home users used to have the "little brother" version of whatever they had at the office. A slower processor, less memory, and a smaller monitor were the common differences, but that's no longer the case. It's the home computer that has all the good stuff now, and the office computer is slow, small, and boring by those standards. Let's take a look at what the differences are.

The typical home computer in 1989 was an IBM Personal Computer/AT or compatible, or its equivalent, with an Intel 80286 processor at a 12-megahertz operating speed, 1 megabyte (1,000,000 characters) of random-access memory, a 40-megabyte hard drive, and a 12-inch color monitor. The typical home computer 90s style (see Figure 1.1) has an Intel 80486 processor cooking along at 50 megahertz, around 4 megabytes of RAM, a 300-megabyte hard drive, a CD-ROM drive, a 15-inch high-resolution color monitor, a modem, and 2.3 children clustered around it.

The typical office computer in 1989 was an Intel 80386 processor at 20 megahertz with 2 megabytes of RAM, a 120-megabyte hard drive, a 14-inch

Figure 1.1 A typical home computer (2.3 children not pictured). Photo courtesy of Packard Bell, Inc.

monitor, and a network connection. The typical office computer in 1995 isn't all that different, and your co-workers may still be using that old '386.

This puts a lot of pressure on the corporate network manager. Every day many John Q. Users stroll into their local network administrator's office and ask, "Why can't I have a 486/more memory/a modem/a CD-ROM drive/Internet access?" The poor network guy's response is a smile, a shrug, and the turning out of empty pockets.

He can only get away with that for so long. Even worse, he can't simply begin acceding to these requests on a one-by-one basis because then he gets the "How come John Q. has all this stuff while I still have my dinky little 386SX?" questions. As they say, "Ya gotta have a plan."

One important thing to realize is that office multimedia is of necessity very different from home multimedia. Take the CD-ROM drive as an example. CD-ROM drives for personal computers can be had for as little as $100, even with the requisite controller card. For the typical office network, which has around 20 PCs, this represents an investment of only a couple of thousand dollars plus the time to install the drives. Easy. Or is it?

Think about the software. Most network-enabled business software is licensed on a "number of simultaneous users" basis. This means that on your 20-station network, if you have five users in WordMulcher at any given time, you only need to purchase five licenses for WordMulcher. But what if WordMulcher is distributed on CD-ROM? Now you have to make a choice. Either buy 20 CD copies so that all users have the program available whenever they need it, or buy the same five copies and establish a library of CDs that have to be checked out every time.

Both options are less than desirable. If you go with the first one, you're spending money you really don't need to for the sake of convenience. If you pick what's behind door number 2, you're now wearing the librarian hat in addition to your many others.

It should be obvious that the "home" concept doesn't work in the *office* setting. Adding CD-ROM to the network has to be done in a centralized fashion. Instead of adding CD-ROM drives to each computer, you add a CD-ROM server to the network and give users access to the server to get to their precious WordMulcher. What shape that server takes and the method of user access are discussed in Chapter 3.

Some components of a multimedia network simply can't be centralized. If you're going to add sound capability to the network, each user is going to need a sound board and a method of reproducing sounds. Speakers? Possibly, but if everyone has speakers on their desks, you could end up with the audible equivalent of Grand Central Station. Headsets might be the better choice.

Other aspects of multimedia that will have to be replicated at the individual workstation: high-quality video and fast video controllers; microphones; motion video decompression (MPEG) cards; and video cameras. These can all work together to empty your wallet quicker than you can say "videoconference."

HEY! WHAT IS AN "OFFICE," ANYWAY?

I f we're going to talk about business computing, we'd better define our terms a little more closely. The concept of a business changed radically in the past twenty years or so, and nowhere is it more evident than in the office.

At the close of World War II life in the United States was based primarily on manufacturing. Large, centralized factories with blue-collar workforces dominated the economic landscape. Farming was the second biggest part of the money-making machine, and service industries ran a very distant third. As our domestic population grew during the post-war era so did the demand for both goods and services. Thus, as manufacturing grew so did the number of people needed to manage, account for, and sell those goods. White-collar workers became much more common, and this is where our traditional concept of the office came from.

Fast distribution by planes, trains, and automobiles provides a wide market for goods and services, so companies are a lot more spread out than they used to be. It isn't uncommon for a company to have its corporate office in one state, its manufacturing facilities in another, and its sales force in yet another. Add to this the incredible explosion of small businesses in the 1980s and 1990s and the latest trend towards working from home. You can see that we're stretching the concept of the office to the breaking point.

Let's take a look at the different meanings for the word office in our current vocabulary. While we're at it we'll discuss the level of computer and multimedia technology likely to be present for each definition.

The Home Office

The smallest possible example of an office is the home office. This is typically an extra room in your apartment, condo, or house that you have outfitted for business rather than personal use.

That doesn't mean that you don't use that room for fun, though. How many of us haven't sat down to write a report and ended up winning a rousing game of Space Blasters? Whatever you do, don't tell the Internal Revenue Service that. Current rules mandate that the home office be as sterile as an operating room if you want to deduct it from your taxes.

The home office computer (see Figure 1.2) is likely to be a pretty advanced machine, comparatively speaking. The reason for this is simple: You're on your own. If the resources you need to complete your work aren't present, you can't run down the hall to borrow Bob's computer, because Bob's not there. The home office computer is likely to have a late-generation processor, lots of RAM, a big hard drive, and an inkjet or personal laser printer.

How about multimedia? Again, probability says that you're better equipped to do multimedia at home than you are at the office. Almost a quarter of all home computers now have CD-ROM drives, for example. Around 10 percent have full multimedia installations, including the CD-ROM card, a sound card, and a set of speakers. As to networked multimedia, you're pretty much (no pun intended) on your own.

Figure 1.2   An advanced home office computer (IBM's) Aptiva. Photo courtesy of
IBM Corporation.

Networking is very difficult to achieve from the home office. It's possible, but requires late-generation hardware, software, and the very best the telephone company has to offer. We're talking about a lot of money to pull the home computer onto the office network, and there aren't too many people doing office work from home, or "telecommuting." However, that's likely to change in the near future, especially in major urban areas.

The Traditional Office

The next step up (or down if you're a stay-at-home sort) in the office hierarchy is the traditional office. It used to be that most offices had one or two computers, and they were rarely hooked together. Moving information from one machine to another was a delicate operation that involved a floppy diskette or two, a fair amount of disruption, and a whole bunch of walking. Nowadays you're likely to walk into an office that has at least one computer per occupant, and those computers are likely to be tied together on a Local Area Network (LAN).

Because the company has to spend a lot of money to buy multiple computers, they're likely to be less lavish with each one, so multimedia features will probably be conspicuously absent. No CD-ROMs, no sound, and certainly no video.

The core computer is likely to be older as well. It will have a processor that is at least one generation back from the state of the art, and a smaller, slower hard drive. What it *does* have is access to the network, which means that some applications that just weren't possible before are present and accounted for, like electronic mail and the ability to share files and programs with co-workers.

This is a pretty succinct description of affairs at most offices in the industrialized nations, especially the offices of contemporary small businesses. As the business grows so does its requirement for office space and eventually for offices. Once you grow beyond a single location you're a candidate for the distributed office.

The Distributed Office

There are actually two different types of distributed office. In the first scenario you've broken the company up into functional units and each unit is in a separate place. An example might be that fictional company we discussed earlier, with Corporate in one city, Manufacturing in another, and Sales in a third. Each group has its own function, but all the groups have to function together for the company to actually get anything useful done.

From an automation standpoint this scenario is likely to look very similar to that of the traditional office when you look at each group as an independent entity, with a number of personal computers on local area networks in each location. However, the individual PCs aren't really anything to write home about. Multimedia features are going to be mostly if not entirely missing as well.

This office is likely to have one major difference from a traditional office. In order for the company to function properly, each of the units has to be able to talk to and share data with the others, so the local area networks are probably going to be tied together across data circuits of one sort or another, becoming a Wide Area Network (WAN). If the information to be shared is minimal, the offices will be loosely tied by slow-speed modems, or if there is a need for constant communication, they could be joined by a higher-speed dedicated circuit or even by some sort of data network.

The second possibility in distributed offices is to have two or more offices that are functionally identical. An example would be a loan company with headquarters in one place and customer offices in several major cities scattered over a state or region. Rather than splitting the functions of the company for greater efficiency, you're duplicating them for better service.

In this case you're still looking at a WAN, but the design is likely to be different. When a company is broken into portions that are geographically distinct, each portion is equally important and needs to communicate with each other portion whenever it's necessary. Thus, the network design is likely to look like a web or a matrix. However, when a company has a central headquarters location and multiple "clone" locations, it is less necessary for the locations to talk to each other and very important that they all talk to headquarters, so the result is likely to be a "star" design (see Figure 1.3).

The Global Office

As with distributed offices, there are really two types of global offices: internal and external. While the term "internal global" seems to be an oxymoron, it really does make sense. What this refers to is single companies or organizations that have broken out of the four walls of the traditional office.

If your job requires that you sit at a desk or in front of a computer screen all day with limited contact with co-workers, customers, or vendors, why should that desk or screen be at the office? It costs money to have you there in the form of rent for the space, utilities, coffee packets for the machine, and so on. Why not work from your home, where the coffee is better?

There are other benefits to working from home. The most obvious one is that it eliminates that terrible drive into the office every morning and the equally horrific drive home. Another is that you don't normally have to dress up to

Figure 1.3 Typical "peer" and "star" distributed office networks.

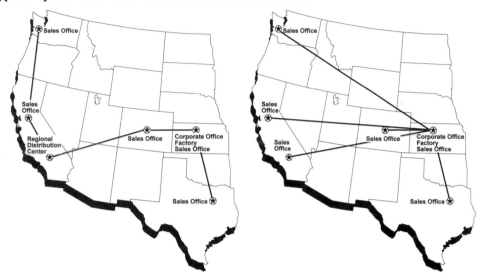

go to work, and as long as you're not using videoconferencing there's no reason why you can't work in an old sweatsuit, a pair of shorts, or even in the buff. Get up in the morning, splash some water on your face, wander into the study, and that's it. You're at work. This concept is called "telecommuting," and it's starting to catch on, largely because of recent improvements in technology.

Many companies have extended computer power into the field by the simple expedient of giving laptop or notebook computers to those who sally forth to do battle in the war of commerce. This newfound portability allows salespeople and managers to continue doing their work whether they're in the office, on a plane, or at home. In order to make this way of working truly efficient, we have to give workers a way to "call the office" with their computers in order to check their mail, gather data files, and send information back to be printed or otherwise acted upon.

That's an internal global office: the functions of a traditional office, but smeared across the landscape in order to save time, money, and wear and tear on the employees.

Let's move on to the external global office. Since we defined the internal global office as a single company network regardless of where the employees are, it makes sense to consider the external global office truly multicompany, multiperson, and multilocation.

At some point in the corporate growth path you will want to reach beyond your own company and make contact with someone else ("Reach out, reach out and touch someone…"). This someone might be a customer, a vendor, or a friend, and the typical way to do this using a computer is via an internetwork. Examples of internetworks include CompuServe, America Online, Prodigy, the forthcoming Microsoft Network, and, of course, the Internet. The first three are examples of commercial internetworks, and the last is a truly public one.

Internetworks provide a means of gathering information for your own use, providing information for the use of others, and communicating with others.

Typically, you don't need Godzilla the Wondercomputer to communicate across internetworks. The speed with which you access the network is likely to be quite low, down in the thousands-of-characters-per-second range. This is quite a difference from the millions of characters per second that in-house networks typically work at, so your computer is likely to find that the bottleneck is outside that attractive beige case.

Internetworks are becoming increasingly graphical, with all the major services providing colorful "point-and-shoot" interfaces to the resources available. However, multimedia across internetworks is likely to be somewhat limited, at least for the time being. Take a look at Chapter 8 to see what the future has in store, though. The times definitely are a'changing.

COLLABORATIVE COMPUTING

O ther than for the pure joy of creating an advanced technology environment, why should we want to do all this? The answer is that it's going to save your company a lot of money and make it leaner, more efficient, and a lot more fun.

The concept is called *collaborative computing*. If we make the basic assumption that two heads can think better than one, then it stands to reason that three, four, or forty heads are really going to improve things. Collaborative computing provides a framework for bringing those heads together, organizing their efforts, managing the process, and producing outstanding results.

Collaborations

Collaborations can occur in two ways. The first way is in real time—in other words, everyone working on the same thing, at the same time, together. The second way is for individuals to work on their own portion in their own time and use some method of pulling all the separate efforts together.

Examples of the first method include whiteboarding applications and video-conferencing. Examples of the second include electronic mail and groupware. We'll give some detailed examples of all of these (and the proverbial "much, much more") as we move through the book.

Collaborative computing is a subversive topic if you're interested in preserving the status quo. Implementing its technologies properly will cause massive changes to the structure of your organization. These applications and components cut across the structure of traditional companies, flattening out the organizational structure as they go. In a truly collaborative environment everyone's contribution is equally important, whether it's from the chairman of the board, a mid-level manager, or a factory worker. If a person is included in the collaborative structure it's for what she can contribute to the project, not for where she is in the corporate food chain.

If you do networked multimedia right, it's likely that you're going to end up with a smaller, tighter company as well. Collaborative computing breaks up bureaucracies like dish soap breaks up grease. It also has a tendency to carry productivity enhancements along with it by its very nature. Let's take a look at why that is.

Leveling the Playing Field

If you work for a traditional company, chances are that your firm is organized along departmental lines, with information created by the lower echelons, riding through the department, and then crossing to other departments through managers and directors. At each level the information is refined, distilled, and condensed into forms that make it more accessible to people outside your specialty.

That methodology works most of the time, but there are some very significant drawbacks. For one thing, you run the risk of losing information that might be valuable to someone outside your department in the distillation process. What you think is unimportant might be of paramount importance to someone else; conversely, what you think is important they might not give two hoots about.

When you move to collaborative computing you move to a team rather than a departmental orientation. Each team member is responsible for his own aspect of the project yet can solicit comments, suggestions, and even share the actual work with anyone else included in the project. Who is doing what and when can be tracked, reported, and managed along the way, and credit is always given where due.

If a company decides to introduce collaborative computing, what does it get for its efforts? There are a number of truly significant benefits, and the only downside is the cost of adding sophisticated hardware and software to the network, along with a pretty fair training requirement. Chief among the benefits is the massively higher productivity of a collaborative environment.

In a departmental hierarchy there is a fair amount of wasted effort. People who produce the detail do so because it's their job, and you have to have the details in order to produce the summaries. Once the summaries are produced, details have a tendency to go by the wayside along with the work required to produce them.

A line manager might take a summary to his boss, who will then produce a summary of the work produced by each of her subordinates, which goes to her boss, and so on. At each level we wash out a bit more of the detail and the underlying work.

Now apply a collaborative computing paradigm. Instead of having to drive information up, over, and then back down the organization, we move it sideways. Individuals at all levels of the company come together to produce a final product that is distributed in the same manner—horizontally; people have to do only the amount of work necessary to satisfy directly the project's requirements—no more and no less. If we hold this concept up to the cold light of reality, we see that applying truly collaborative concepts to the organization can result in a significantly reduced need for managers and/or supervisors.

In other words, if you sign on for the complete treatment and follow through on implementing collaborative computing the way it's supposed to be done, you're looking at a choice: You can either reduce the number of people working for your company or shift them into other positions with additional collaborative benefits, and really give the competition a run for its money.

This brings us to the second major benefit of collaborative computing: reduced costs. We'll look at these in detail in Chapter 5, but despite what can be a very hefty tab for full implementation of networked multimedia, the cost savings from using it to do collaborative computing are so large that, regardless of what you do, it will pay for itself very quickly.

And there's yet a third reason to go to the collaborative computing environment. It makes work more fun. Electronic mail doesn't have to be just words on a screen. How would you like to open a document and have it talk to you? Or look at another one and have it look back? Sound- and video-enabled e-mail offer just that, and more. Once this stuff is in place, you know that people won't restrict it to business use only. Sooner or later, the day will come when you open your mail and it sings *Happy Birthday* to you, off key and warbling badly as only the gang down the hall can do it, and then you'll know you've arrived.

A Day in the Life...

For the sake of argument let's assume that you have a great job at a great company with bosses who are as in love with technology as you are. You have been allowed to plan, purchase, and implement every single piece of multimedia hardware and software your heart desires, and your network is the stuff of dreams. What might a typical day be like?

Your alarm clock goes off at 6 A.M. Like most of us, you slap the snooze bar a couple of times and then groggily heave yourself out of bed and off to the shower. A few minutes later you are clean and mostly awake, and you decide to log in to the network from home while the coffee is brewing.

You drift into the study and power-on the computer. A few seconds later your ISDN modem is establishing a 128-kilobit-per-second link with the office communications server, and you are ready to log in. The login script informs you that there are six new pieces of e-mail in your in-box, including two voice messages, a video message, and a fax. You groan. Work starts early today.

Starting up the mail program, you note that one of the standard e-mail messages has a 2-megabyte attachment. That must be the WordMulcher update you've been waiting for. You need to have this update at home, so you click on the e-mail message with your mouse, and 45 seconds later you have the update file. Next, you look at the other standard e-mails and reply to each with a quick note.

Now, you accidentally click on one of the video messages. A box pops up on screen that says, "You are attached via a slow link. This is a video message, and will probably not be understandable at this transmission rate. Do you want to continue?" Grateful for the opportunity to back out gracefully, you click on the No button.

The coffee's ready, so you log out and power-off the system. You'll finish those messages when you get to work, and you're glad to have made a start on it. A hasty breakfast, and into "appropriate business attire," and it's off to the car with you.

While you're making the morning commute, your pager goes off. Checking the alphanumeric display, you see that it's yet another e-mail message, but the sender tagged it "urgent," and your mail filtering rules send such messages out via the pager link. *Hmmm.* Yep, this one is important. One of your co-workers can't seem to get his videophone working, and he's expecting a call from the San Francisco office at any time. You pick up the cellular phone, and after a few pointed questions it becomes apparent that the cleaning people accidentally disconnected the video camera's feed line last night. He snaps, twists, and pops the connector back on, and all is well.

At last, traffic begins to clear and you make the rest of the run in to the office in record time. Out of the car, across the lot, up the steps, and into your tasteful but understated office. Your desktop computer is already on, but being a security-conscious sort, you logged off and locked the keyboard last night, so you have to log back in.

As soon as you do, the script informs you that three new e-mails have arrived. You start the mail program and decide to deal with the older messages first. When you click on the first of the two video e-mails, a small (3-by-3-inch) window opens on screen and the recorded face of your CEO appears. He tells you that because of the wonderful things you've done with the network this year, the board of directors has decided to increase your operating budget by 30 percent for the next fiscal year. Grinning like a maniac, you decide that a more somber written note of appreciation is in order, and you rattle off a quick but heartfelt reply.

Just before you open the next video message your computer begins beeping and the InterPhone control box pops up on top of your e-mail program. A friend is calling from Sweden across the Internet. Picking up the microphone, you discuss the professional basketball game he saw via satellite last night. Marveling at the fact that this is a free transatlantic "phone" call, you talk for a few minutes about sports trivia, the weather, and your respective love lives. You conclude the call and return to your e-mail.

The next video e-mail is from your assistant at the Dallas office. She reports that they have been having problems getting information in a timely manner out of Los Angeles and wonders what you want to do about it. Since you've been looking for an excuse to convert that part of the network to Frame Relay for greater reliability, this seems to be the perfect opportunity. Clicking on the Reply Video box, you address a few remarks to the camera, asking your assistant to collect some reliability statistics and forward them to you as soon as she can.

The last e-mail is from the brand new office in Kuala Lumpur, Malaysia. The text message from the office manager there says that he wants several additional computers. You know that the Kuala Lumpur office is on a dial-up link and that transmissions are delayed both by the speed of the link and by the fact that it's 14 hours later there, but you decide to reply by voice anyway. You click on "Reply Voice" and dictate a short response, asking that the office manager reply by voice e-mail as well to test the system.

As you're getting ready to walk down to the server room, your computer beeps again, but it's not the InterPhone beep. This is the office videoconferencing system. You return to your desk, and the videophone control box is the top window, announcing a call from the Vice-President of Sales . You click "Answer," and his face appears in a full-screen window.

He wants to know if the company can provide videoconferencing capability to his favorite customer in Minneapolis. You explain that right now video-conferencing is only available across your private wide area network in order to save costs, but that you expect to add ISDN access (and you carefully explain what ISDN is) early next year. At that time his customer can buy the necessary hardware and software and call him up at any time. The Sales guy thanks you and terminates the call.

The rest of the morning is uneventful. A few phone calls (how old fashioned), a couple of visits from subordinates and superiors, and it's time for lunch.

Upon your return from lunch, you walk into the office just as the videophone control box pops up on your screen. It's the human resources manager, and she wants to talk about the personnel requisition you just submitted for a salesperson in Los Angeles. She has questions about several of the experience requirements you put on the form. Since the form was electronically generated in the e-mail program, you call it up and paste it into the whiteboard section of the videoconferencing software so you can both look at it and mark it up. She uses her mouse to circle a section that doesn't make sense to her, and you quickly type in a revised requirement that satisfies both of you. The task finished, she terminates the call and you return to your electronic paperwork.

Moving to the word-processing program, you rattle off a memo on production delays of your company's hottest new product. Pulling down the File...E-Mail menu, you ship the memo off to all concerned without even leaving the word-processing program. Two more memos, some time surfing the Internet looking for a new recipe to try out at home tonight, and it's time to go home.

Let's take stock. During this day you exchanged information with around twenty people. Half of these exhanges were simple textual electronic mail. Two were voice-enabled e-mail, maintaining the personal contact but conserving precious bandwidth. There were three video e-mails and two videoconferences, saving you the trouble of leaving your office and walking to and from other people's offices. Three actual visits in person from various co-workers and one personal phone call via the Internet complete the mix.

Fantasy? Only in that many of us could not afford to implement all of these components right now. Every single element of this idyllic day at the office is currently available as described and could be integrated into a complete, cohesive state-of-the-art network tomorrow. A veritable smorgasbord of tasty technologies, but we have to pick and choose to come up with the most cost-effective solutions.

In the following chapters we'll discuss the levels of multimedia implementations available, the infrastructure changes necessary to support those technologies, and the benefits that can be expected to accrue from each.

2 COMPONENTS OF NETWORKED MULTIMEDIA— SOFTWARE

There are a tremendous number of options available for adding multimedia to the network. If you look at multimedia as a Chinese restaurant menu, from which you choose individual pieces from hither and yon, you can create a confusing mixture of technologies and techniques. Sometimes it's better to take a layered approach, so we'll look at the components of multimedia software and hardware from the entry-level, the midrange, and the high-end "take no prisoners" perspectives.

THE ENTRY LEVEL

Networked multimedia at the entry level is usually a pretty simple affair. It should be light on the wallet, easy to implement, and easy to integrate into the organization. Even if you were one of those semimythical megamillionaires who could afford to implement a complete networked-multimedia installation in a single step, you probably wouldn't want to, simply because, despite how unutterably *neat* all this stuff is, the culture shock would likely stunt your company's growth for years. Better to ease into it by picking projects that have a quick payback and that users will embrace, enjoy, and find useful in their daily routines.

Whiteboards

Okay, we've managed to whet your appetite for networked multimedia. What can you do now, for a minimal investment and with no hardware upgrade necessary? The answer is *whiteboards*.

How often have you been talking with someone on the phone and said to yourself, "Jeez! I really wish I could show this person exactly what I'm talking about"? Well, you can, and it's pretty easy to do. Whiteboard programs are commercially available, inexpensive, and easy to install and use.

What is a whiteboard? It is a way to share screens, keystrokes, and mouse movements between two or more computers. Let's say that a friend calls you and asks how to perform a particular function in WordMulcher for Windows. Instead of doing the usual, which is to call up WordMulcher on your own computer, do the thing that she's asking about, and talk her through the keystrokes and mouse movements, you start the whiteboard application and establish a connection to the whiteboard on her computer.

Now you can see her WordMulcher screen. You still have her on the phone, so you're talking to her as you show her the menu item that she wanted, how to select the various options, and how to format her selection. You think that a particular part of the process is very important, so for emphasis you select the pointer function and draw a circle around that part of the screen. Because this emphasis is part of the whiteboard application rather than WordMulcher, you can do this without interfering with the process. You can share text, graphics, programs, and data with any of your whiteboard-enabled users in this way.

In fact, your friend says, "You know, Audrey over at the Purchasing desk was asking me about this just yesterday. Can you show her how to do this too?" You reply "Sure!" and instruct the whiteboard application to link Audrey's PC into the two that are already talking. You undo the changes you've made and let your friend demonstrate to both you and Audrey that they have learned how to do what they asked for. Once everyone is happy you close the whiteboard application, hang up the phone, and everyone goes their merry way.

Whiteboards can be very effective productivity tools, especially in the technical support and training arenas. They provide multiple-user support simultaneously, reduce the need to actually travel to users' desks or sites to help them out, and, because they're completely interactive, you get immediate feedback on whether the person or persons at the other end really understand what's going on.

Whiteboards can also be extremely useful for brainstorming sessions. Several people can construct lists of issues or action items from the comfort of their own offices, with access to all the support materials that are already at their fingertips. Also, big meetings, where people have to break out of their schedules and move to a meeting room (which is all too often in another building or even another city), are eliminated. All you need is a PC, the whiteboarding application, and a telephone.

Most whiteboard applications use either Microsoft Windows or IBM OS/2 as the base operating system. Since both Windows and OS/2 will run DOS environments and the programs that run in them, you can also use whiteboards for these. Accounting programs, old-style word-processing programs, and databases are examples of this regressive program class.

Whiteboarding applications aren't expensive, either. Expect a whiteboard package for use on a single local area network to cost less than $1,000. If you have a wide area network, you'll pay that same $1,000 per server up to around the five-server level, and then you'll start to see price breaks.

Sound-Enabled Electronic Mail

So far in this chapter we've talked about a multimedia application that requires no hardware at all. Now we're going to talk about one that is still considered entry level but requires hardware at every PC on the network. Even though it requires modifications to all your workstations, adding sound to e-mail is a low-cost way to give the network multimedia functionality. All it takes is a sound board, some speakers, and a microphone.

A low-end sound board uses an inexpensive chip called an FM synthesizer to create computer-generated music and voice. The quality ranges from acceptable to good. Better-quality sound boards ($300 and up) use Wave Tables, which are digital recordings of actual sounds stored in read only memory on the sound board. Some boards store up to 2 megabytes of digitized sounds, and the quality is noticeably better than that of the synthesized types.

To record the spoken voice, an external microphone is used and the recording is stored digitally as a Wave file. The Wave file name usually ends with the extension .WAV. These files can be very large, depending on the fidelity with which the speech was recorded. A three-minute voice recording at 22 kilohertz (average fidelity) will result in a file of approximately 3 megabytes. Regrettably, most programs that store and record voice do not use compression, so that is the file size stored on the PC or network.

By the way, here's a technology that requires a hardware purchase, but usually no software! If you're already using a Microsoft Windows- or Macintosh-based personal computer, the odds are that your e-mail application already supports sound. How? Object Linking and Embedding, or OLE for short.

Every Windows installation comes with a mini-application called the Sound Recorder (Figure 2.1). This allows users with a sound board to record spoken speech through a standard cheap microphone available at any Radio Shack for less than $10. To add a voice message to e-mail, the user calls up the sound

Figure 2.1 The Windows Sound Recorder.

recorder, records a message, and then drags the message to the e-mail program and drops it in. The e-mail is addressed and sent in the normal way.

When the recipient gets the message, he sees an enclosed sound file. Using the mouse to double-click on the sound file automatically starts the media player, which then plays the message. The user can discard or retain the sound file either separately or as part of the e-mail. It's just that simple.

So you're going to need a sound board with speakers and a microphone in every Windows-capable workstation that will be used for e-mail. Seems like a lot of money, doesn't it? If you think so, you haven't looked at the price of sound boards lately. You can buy one of reasonable quality (and remember that you don't need any better than reasonable quality, as these boards will only be used for voice recording) for as little as $50. Cheap desktop speakers will cost you an additional $20, and a microphone is $10 or less. The total outlay is $80 per station, or around $3,000 to equip a complete 40 station network. As we say in California, "kewl, dude!"

Well, we don't really talk that way in California. We only do that when we think New Yorkers might be listening.

There is another tangible benefit to sound enabling. If you have already added CD-ROM to the network or are about to, you now have the ability to provide more of what the CD-ROM is good for to everyone on the network. Lots of CD-ROM software these days contains an audible component, usually in the form of music that accompanies games and spoken words that accompany tutorials and such. With sound at the workstation your users can take full advantage of this, assuming they have the software to do so, of course. They may very well already have that ability. Most presentation graphics programs are able to play back .WAV files during a presentation, and, as we discussed, you can add sound to any application that is OLE-enabled, including (paradoxically) word-processing programs.

Just as with CD-ROM, there is a downside to this capability. You may be asking for trouble on the network itself. Excluding the cost per workstation of providing quality recording and playback capability, remember that the recorded files are likely to be large. This means that you're going to need to look at server hard-disk space to make sure that there's going to be enough room to store all those sound-clip files.

Network bandwidth (the overall "raw" information-carrying capacity) will also need to be examined. A regular old Ethernet network typically offers around 400,000 bytes per second of throughput to the workstation, so a 3-minute sound clip of 3 megabytes will take almost 8 seconds of bandwidth to be played back. If you have a lot of users and a lot of sound, faster or more sophisticated network topologies might very well be called for.

Multimedia Presentation Graphics

Presentation graphics programs have been around for quite some time. There have been versions available for mainframe computers for over 20 years, and some of the earliest programs for PCs fell into this category as well.

As personal computers got faster and the operating systems for them became more sophisticated, so too did the presentation graphics programs. The earliest programs were really nothing more than slide projectors. You designed each screen independently of the others, and moving from one screen to the next was a routine and unexciting event.

As this class of program improved, the transitions from one "slide," as each individual screen in a presentation is called, to the next became more exciting. Wipe, fade, lap, and dissolve transitions made the slide show more of a process than an unconnected series of events.

The goal was quite a bit more lofty than that, however. The standard against which presentation graphics are measured is the actual slide show. If all you have is a single slide projector, it's pretty easy to measure presentation graphics programs favorably against it. But what about professional presentations using noncomputer multimedia?

Marketing and visual presentation specialists call a whole range of tools into play when crafting a multimedia presentation. Multiple slide projectors, often as many as ten at a time, are employed, along with music, sound effects, and lights, to create an atmosphere and a mood. This is what multimedia presentation graphics programs compete against.

Late-generation programs compete pretty effectively, too. Coupled with a fast processor, high-quality sound cards, and fast video, you can create a multimedia presentation that compares favorably with a professionally produced stage show at a fraction of the cost.

The key to creating an attention-grabbing presentation is the effective use of movement. If your presentation is perceived as static, you are creating too many opportunities for people's minds to wander away during it.

There are many ways to bind a collection of static images or text into a seamless presentation, and good multimedia presentation graphics give you the tools to employ all of them.

The simplest is to use transitions between images. As we discussed earlier, programs from a few years back offered that capability. Why simply replace one slide with another when with minimal effort the replacement can slide, bump, push, or dissolve into the original? The transition itself becomes a part of the presentation, and people watch to see how the transitions are accomplished.

But people can be flighty, and we need to employ other methods of holding their attention. Music is also an effective method of binding presentations together, and again, late-generation presentation graphics programs have several different types of music-making capability.

The simplest of these capabilities is to play back recorded sound, whether music, someone's voice, or the sound of rain hitting the cobblestones of a Viennese park. To record sounds like these all you need is a source, a sound board, a Wave recorder program, and lots of hard-disk space. Let me repeat that: *lots* of hard disk space.

The source is easy. It can be an audio CD, a radio, or your voice recorded with a microphone. The sound board is also easy, and the cost is minimal. In the next chapter we take a look at different types of sound boards and their relative costs. The Wave recorder program is the easiest of all. If you have an IBM-compatible personal computer with Microsoft Windows or OS/2, or an Apple Macintosh, you have everything you need to capture sound because this program came with the operating system of the computer you own.

Before recording you'll have to decide just how good the sound quality should be. Voice can be recorded on a single channel at 22 kilohertz for a respectable level of quality, and it'll only cost you around 1.3 megabytes per minute. If you want full-fidelity stereo at 44 kilohertz on each channel, be prepared to store 10.3 megabytes per minute! The most common compromise is to go with 22 kilohertz per channel in stereo. Using these values will require around 6 megabytes of space per minute of recorded audio.

This sounds pretty good to most people because the range of human hearing is right around that number: from 18 to 24 kilohertz, depending on the individual. That difference in hearing range is why some people adore classical music and others don't understand what the big deal is.

Is there an alternative to these incredible storage requirements? Of course there is. The Musical Instrument Device Interface (MIDI) offers a very good way to store incredibly high-quality audio in impressively tiny spaces.

There is a catch, however. MIDI can *only* be used to store music; if you want voice or most sound effects, you'll probably have to go back to Wave files because MIDI doesn't store the actual sounds. Instead, it stores information about those sounds and uses it to recreate them on either the original instruments or other devices. Every time you use a MIDI instrument such as a piano-style keyboard to make a sound, that sound generates events. Pressing the A Sharp key generates a Note-On event, and releasing it generates a Note-Off event. Information about the instrument and the events you created with it are what's stored in the MIDI file, not the actual music.

This has several advantages. The first is that, because all you're recording are the events, MIDI files are very, very small. A 10-minute recording of a five-piece band could be stored in as little as 200,000 bytes of space with perfect fidelity, because playback is simply commanding the instruments to do it all over again.

The second advantage is that you don't have to play the file back onto the original instruments. Any MIDI-capable instrument or sound board will do; the quality of the instrument or sound board used controls the quality of the playback. For a discussion of different types of sound board and their respective benefits and liabilities, take a look in Chapter 3.

The next step in maintaining people's attention is to add motion to the presentation. Transitions do add value, but in this video age people are accustomed to seeing things *happen* on the screen, so you'll need to look at the different levels of adding movement. The simplest is to add animation.

Animation can be as basic as a mouse cursor sliding across a simulated screen and clicking a simulated button, or as complex as fully rendered cartoon people striding across the screen and stopping to discuss a point with the audience. Your design skills and budget will be the only limiting factors.

Simple animations can be created by hand in most multimedia presentation programs, or they can be created by having the program watch over your shoulder (electronically speaking) as you perform a task and the program stores your actions. More complex presentations will require the use of either a sophisticated animation program or a professional designer, or both.

When you use another program to create an animation, it will usually end up as a video file of the AVI, FLI, or QuickTime format, depending on the tools you use. Once the file has been created you can drop it right into your presentation using either of two methods: built-in tools or embedded objects.

Figure 2.2   Macromedia's Director.

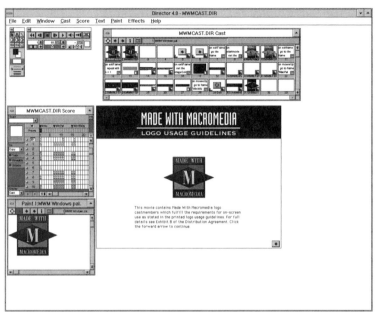

Some presentation graphics programs, like Macromedia's Director (Figure 2.2), have all the design and playback tools built in. You manipulate the program directly to create your complete multimedia presentation. Others use system functions to take contributions from multiple programs and bind them together for the final result. Director is a very powerful (and quite costly) tool for creating professional multimedia applications. If you don't need all the horsepower but still want to put together something that will impress the Board of Directors, take a look at Director's little brother, Action! Action! has about 75 percent of the features found in Director, which still makes it a very powerful program.

Microsoft's Powerpoint (Figure 2.3) is one of the latter type. Powerpoint is OLE enabled, so you'll just call up an application included with Windows called the Media Player, attach your audio or video file to the player, and drag it onto your presentation to be dropped in place. It's as simple as that. When the presentation gets to the point that you've attached multimedia components with OLE, it will automatically execute and play or display those components.

Figure 2.3   Microsoft Powerpoint presentation with embedded audio and video objects.

THE MIDDLE RANGE

Once your entry-level applications are implemented, everyone's trained and happy, and some of the productivity benefits are starting to be seen, you can begin to look at some of the midrange multimedia components available to you. These middle-of-the-road items promise even greater jumps in productivity and user satisfaction, but also require quite bit more in terms of planning, implementation, and user training processes.

When you make the commitment to midrange collaborative computing, you're also looking at making parts of your company's infrastructure collaborative as well. Computers will talk to each other without user intervention, telephones will talk to computers, and, hopefully, people will talk to each other.

There's a big gap between low-end and midrange networked multimedia. What you can accomplish at the low end with very few dollars takes a lot more work at the middle end, and a lot more money. A cost–benefit analysis will tell you fairly quickly whether these technologies are desirable for your network.

Video-Enabled Electronic Mail

If the last step in low-end multimedia is sound enabled e-mail, then the next step is surely video-enabled e-mail. What is it going to take? Hardware and software at every workstation on the network but at varying levels.

First, you have to realize that not every person in the company needs the ability to *create* video e-mail but that everyone should have the ability to *view* it. Those who are only going to need to view video e-mail will need only the sound board that we (hopefully) already gave them for sound-enabled e-mail. They'll also need a video playback program, such as Microsoft's Video for Windows or the Macintosh QuickTime player.

Video for Windows is an OLE-enabled program, so video clips will simply appear as an enclosure in regular e-mail which the recipient has only to double-click on to play it back. Performance should be acceptable on any PC with a 25-Megahertz processor or better, including Intel 80386-based processors.

People who will be creating the video e-mail are another story entirely. They're going to need a raft of features, including software, a camera, and a video capture board. The investment can be anywhere from $1,000 to $4,000 per workstation, with $2,000 the current average. Prices are expected to drop, however, and by late 1996 the price to play should be in the $1,000 range for good-quality equipment.

There's an interesting side benefit to using video-enabled e-mail as opposed to merely sound enabled. Remember that we said that the current storage methods for sound don't have any kind of compression associated with them? That's not true for video. There are currently four major standards for recorded video on microcomputers, and all four incorporate on-the-fly compression. When you compress the video sound comes along for the ride.

The most common method of storing motion video is called MPEG, named after the Moving Picture Expert Group that defined the standard. MPEG video can be played back on a standard IBM-compatible PC without any special hardware (as long as the PC is a speedy one), but it takes special equipment to record, compress, and store the video "clip." If you use a software program to compress and decompress images, called a CODEC (Coder/Decoder), performance is acceptable on a wide range of equipment; however, in order to achieve good performance, the image size is reduced. The usual size for playing back MPEG images using software alone is only 300×200 pixels. If you need better performance or larger displayed images, there are two flavors of add-in expansion boards available.

The first type is a full CODEC that uses a coprocessor to both compress and decompress MPEG video as it is either captured or replayed. Images can be displayed at 30 frames per second (TV speed) at sizes all the way up to full screen. MPEG boards don't actually display images. Instead, they attach to the VGA board already in your computer by attaching a cable to the "feature connector" on the video board (Bet you never expected to actually use one of those, did you?).

Expect an MPEG board with full CODEC to set you back around $2,000. If all you are going to do is play back MPEG at 30 frames per second and in full-screen mode, then all you need is an MPEG player board. This type of board has only the decoder circuitry and is a lot cheaper. Good-quality boards from domestic companies will cost around $200 each, and several overseas companies were displaying MPEG players at the COMDEX computer trade show in Las Vegas for as low as $80 each.

Why are these sophisticated boards so inexpensive? Because all they have is the ability to take a digital stream, decompress it, and turn it into video information. They don't actually have to display the information. The MPEG board is connected directly to that feature connector on the VGA card, so video information is turned over in a "raw" state to the display card, which then goes through the process of turning it into displayable images. This is an admirable division of responsibilities, in which everything works properly and serves to keep prices low as well.

So how do you add video to e-mail? The same way that we described adding sound. The video equipment will come with a recorder application that may even give you some limited editing capabilities. Simply call up the recording software, say your piece (remember, smile for the camera!), and store the video. The software (and hardware if you have it) will compress the video and store it in a file with the extension .MPG. Using OLE's "drag and drop," carry the file into your e-mail, address it as usual, and fire it off.

When the addressee receives it, he simply double-clicks on the icon representing the video. If his computer is properly equipped, the MPEG player software will start, call up the file, and play it back. If the computer doesn't have the proper software, then a polite little Windows message will appear saying, "There is no application associated with the selected file."

You can send the same video to more than one person simply by addressing it to everyone you want to send it to. Every known e-mail program supports this, and the good ones don't make multiple copies of the file on the same server, thus freeing up valuable disk space.

The second major method of acquiring and playing back video comes from Intel corporation and its Indeo system. Indeo works exactly the same way that MPEG does, except that the storage format is Intel proprietary. We could argue all day over which one is more efficient or quicker, but the bottom line is that they're both within rock-throwing distance of each other. Indeo is slightly more expensive, but there is one very good reason that you might choose it over MPEG. Video recording is a small portion of what Indeo does; the rest is Intel's solution for videoconferencing, and it's a very good solution indeed. More detail on videoconferencing can be found later in this chapter, in the section "The High End."

For Macintoshes and Apple Power PCs, Apple provides QuickTime, which has the benefit of being playable on IBM compatibles with Windows. Quick-Time is the least space-efficient of the three, but it does provide a smooth playback from software only, even on lower-end PCs.

The fourth standard, called H.320, is the only true standard of the four, having been created and ratified by the European telecommunication standards organization CCITT. H.320 is also different from the other three in that it is designed solely for real-time videoconferencing rather than for storage of recorded files for later playback. You can "capture" an H.320 session, but it's not particularly fast or efficient to do so. If you're thinking about starting with video e-mail and then later upgrading to the complete videoconferencing suite, then H.320-based systems probably won't be for you.

When deciding what components to install where, you can be picky about it. Who gets the full treatment, including both recording and playback capability, and who gets playback capability only? For those who get playback only you can decide whether to implement it in hardware with an MPEG player board or to install the software only. The cost–benefit analysis can be a little tricky, since some people that you would not ordinarily think of as needing "the good stuff" would actually take great benefit from it. We'll talk about this in detail in Chapter 5.

Groupware

Explaining the concept of groupware is probably the hardest thing about it. Groupware takes the best of three separate technologies, binds them together across a network, and adds a platform for future expansion. The three technologies are electronic mail, document storage and retrieval, and an application development environment that allows you to manipulate the first two technologies and add additional components.

To be a true groupware product a program should use a client/server architecture with a central information repository and individual clients capable of manipulating and adding to the repository.

The best known member of the groupware category is Lotus (now IBM's Lotus) Notes. This is actually a suite of programs all bound together by a common platform, in this case the Notes server. There are two things that make Notes a unique product: the extensibility of its environment and its ability to eliminate redundancies in information storage. Each of these features deserves further explanation.

Notes is incredibly extensible. You can choose to use the "native" programming tools to build your own applications that run entirely within Notes, or you can build external applications (assuming that you're a pretty good programmer) that communicate with Notes through its Applications Programming Interface (API). Lotus has a number of applications built in this fashion, some for sale as separate products and some included in the basic package.

One of the most severe problems involved in information storage is the tremendously redundant amount of data stored on the network. Often, this redundancy is completely hidden from the users who created it in the first place, and it is almost impossible to either locate or eliminate it using "normal" network tools. Here's an example.

Let's say that you have a spreadsheet that you want to e-mail to a co-worker. You make your final changes, save the spreadsheet, and leave the program that you used to make the changes. You start up the electronic mail program, type a quick note to your co-worker, and attach the spreadsheet file. Or did you?

Actually, what you did was instruct the e-mail program to make a copy of your spreadsheet and store it as an attachment to the e-mail. There are now two copies of your spreadsheet on the network server: your original and the copy stored in the e-mail system.

Later your colleague receives a notification that she has mail. She starts the e-mail program and sees that it's a note from you along with an attached file. She reads the note and saves the attached file in her spreadsheet directory, but decides not to delete the e-mail just in case she needs to save the file again. Now there are three copies of that spreadsheet on the network: yours, hers, and the copy stored in the e-mail system.

Two days later you're cleaning out your e-mail boxes, and you decide to delete the e-mail and the spreadsheet attachment that you sent earlier. Did that delete the copy in the e-mail system? Nope, because both your e-mail and your co-worker's are pointing at that file, and it won't be deleted until she decides to delete it, if she ever does. It can get even worse. Some electronic mail systems are more than a little fragile, and they can forget about links to attached files all too easily. When that happens, you're left with an orphan file in the e-mail directory with a cryptic name like 055a67b8.ca3. You have no way of knowing whose file it is or was, and deleting any of those files is something you do at your considerable peril.

So what do Notes and its ilk do for you? This is one of the greatest strengths of Notes and simultaneously its greatest weakness. Notes maintains a personal computer called a Notes server, completely distinct from your network server. This PC uses the latest version of the OS/2 operating system to run a document management database that jealously protects both the data and the client programs' relationships with it. This becomes doubly important when you consider the nature of several of the add-on applications available for Notes.

The Notes database is fully relational, which means that everything stored on a Notes server appears on that server once and once only. Notes servers store shared document databases for spreadsheet data, presentations, scanned images, electronic mail, faxes, and other business documents.

This design can be a weakness because it means that you're going to have to add at least one server to your network for each site using Notes. Since these servers use OS/2 as the operating system, the probability is that you're going to have to learn how to install, configure, and maintain yet another type of network server and the applications that run on it. Challenges abound in this industry, don't they?

Notes clients (the programs that run on users' workstations and connect to the server) allow the Notes server to manage the storage of their information through OLE. Just as with other OLE-enabled electronic mail programs, adding a voice message or a video clip is as simple as "drag and drop," but in this case you're dropping it onto a separate server that makes sure your message gets where it's going and is not unnecessarily duplicated.

Two of the add-on applications for Notes deal directly with networked multimedia. Phone Notes allows users to operate Lotus Notes applications from touch-tone telephones anywhere in the world, without needing a computer with them. This can extend the Notes environment applications to non-Notes users for things like inquiring into order status or looking up a person's name or phone number, or almost anything else that can be managed across a phone line. Information that people enter using touch-tone phones either at the keypad or by voice recording can be stored in Notes, too, which makes it good for setting appointments or taking surveys.

Lotus Video for Notes provides the ability to store and retrieve digital video in Notes documents. One interesting thing that Notes does that other programs don't is take a single frame from the video and use it as a "poster" to indicate what's in the video message. Clicking on the poster plays the video. The tools to record, edit, and play back your videos are built into Video Notes, so unlike with video-enabled e-mail, you don't need an external program to start the process. Since the video clips are stored in the Notes server's database, they are in one place only, and if you have a powerful enough server, it can play the same clip or a number of different clips simultaneously for up to 40 users on an Ethernet network.

How valuable can Notes be to the collaborative enterprise? Valuable enough for IBM Corporation to plunk down several billion dollars to purchase Notes' developer, Lotus Development Corporation. IBM's stated intention is to continue to enhance the Notes product and to develop additional add-ons that will enhance the collaborative environment.

Bob, It's Your Computer on Line 6...

A new topic in business management circles is Computer–Telephone Integration, or CTI for short. CTI used to be exclusively the province of the very largest companies, with telephone systems of excruciating complexity costing hundreds of thousands of dollars hooked to mainframe computer systems costing...well, you don't even want to think about it.

To put it in Las Vegas terms, CTI has come to the three-dollar blackjack table. You can actually implement it at the desktop for less than $200 per station, if your area of the country has Caller ID. This is a service provided by the telephone company that lets a telephone call arrive with a digital "header" that contains the telephone number of the calling party. If you set things up so that your computer snags that header just as the phone rings, you can pick up the receiver just as the caller's data files show up on your screen.

If you have an 800 or 900 number, you don't even need Caller ID. All calls dialed to these numbers have Automatic Number Identification (ANI), which the phone company needs to know how to bill the call. When your bill arrives, it shows the originating number, the length of the call, and the amount it cost. Don't believe me? Pick up the phone, call 1-800-MY-ANI-IS, and listen to what the computer tells you.

By the way, it's considered extremely bad form to answer the phone with "Well, Hello, Mr. Jones! Would you like to order another set of Athletic Supporters today?" even if you know that (a) it's Mr. Jones and (b) he's ordered three sets of athletic supporters in the past six months. That kind of knowledge has a tendency to frighten and intimidate people and in all probability, it's one of your customers you're talking to, and the last thing you want to do is frighten him. It's better to have him say, "Hello, this is Mr. Jones," at which point you can say, "Mr. Jones! Great to hear from you! We haven't heard from you since late February!" This will make Mr. Jones think that (a) you thought he was important enough that you remembered him and (b) you missed him.

There are two methods of bringing CTI to the desktop. You can hook up your desktop computer directly to the telephone using either the phone's built-in serial port or an interface box if your phone doesn't have one. However, this can be an expensive way to do CTI, as it requires hardware at every workstation. The hardware can be pretty darned expensive, too. Consider Northern Telecom's Meridian series, for example. All Meridian 1 telephones have the option of installing a serial data port that operates at up to 19,200 bits per second, at the "minimal" price of $249 per telephone. AT&T, Rolm, Fujitsu, and Siemens all have similar options.

If you're adding desktop-based CTI to a company with a large centralized phone system, like Northern Telecom or its ilk, be prepared to spend around $500 per station. This includes the cost of the station adapter, the extra boards you're going to have to add to the switch itself to support these adapters, and some minor programming changes.

If you work for a smaller company, you actually get a break. There are a number of manufacturers of adapter boxes that attach between the telephone's wall jack and the actual telephone, and also hook into your computer's serial or parallel port. One such company, OCTuS, sells the Personal Telecommunications Adapter (PTA) for use with single- or dual-line telephones for less than $200. These adapters work with some (but not all) small-company PBXs. The rule of thumb is that if your PBX says "Digital Switch" somewhere on it, then you cannot use these adapters, as they only work with analog systems—which is to say, standard business lines including Centrex. Yes, even the very smallest companies can have CTI!

The software to support tying the individual telephone to the individual PC, is from Microsoft, and it's called the Telephony Applications Programming Interface (TAPI). TAPI provides a "framework" for programmers to work within, and you can either purchase software that supports it or build your own. The latter option can be useful if you have unusual software requirements, like a very specific order-entry system that must be built to your specifications.

There is another way to achieve "real" CTI, though. If you have a Novell NetWare network, Novell offers its Telephony Services Applications Programming Interface, or TSAPI. TSAPI ties the telephone switch to the network server, not the phone to the individual PC. This means that hooking the network to the phone system is only going to take one piece of hardware (in the switch) and three pieces of software (one in the phone switch, one in the network server, and one in the desktop PC). The network server takes care of synchronizing the ringing of the phone with the displaying of data, and the user doesn't have to muck about with cables and connectors.

Deciding to use TSAPI may very well be the most cost-effective choice, especially for very large CTI installations. Expect to pay between $10,000 and $15,000 to put the technology into the telephone switch, about $5,000 for each network server you need to hook up, and nothing at all (other than the cost of TSAPI-enabled applications software) for the desktops.

Having TAPI- or TSAPI-enabled software is the real kicker. Simply putting the computer and the telephone together isn't going to buy you a lot. Capturing the caller information, storing it, and then being able to recall it upon demand is only a gateway to more productive work. The actual benefit comes from having applications software that provides useful information to the person who answers the phone, and allows her to capture and store additional useful information about that caller for the next call.

The High End

S o you're going to do it. You've decided to grab that brass ring after all and go for the ultimate in collaborative computing—the interactive, real-time data, voice, and video network of your dreams. Why? Because, believe it or not, it's going to save money and time for your organization. Travel is virtually eliminated, people are closer to each other despite geographic separations, mistakes are reduced (but never eliminated), and people feel better about who they are, what they do, and where they do it. That last part usually translates into higher productivity, and all of a sudden real time means real dollars.

All of the technologies that we have discussed so far can run on 80 percent of the networks currently installed. No infrasystem upgrades are necessary, as far as the local area network is concerned, to support them. Several needed new workstation goodies and many others may very well require that you increase hard-disk storage or add components to the server, but nothing that would cause farreaching changes. Sorry, time's up.

Videoconferencing

Videoconferencing is a bandwidth stealer. You can get away with doing point-to-point videoconferencing across an Ethernet LAN (more on LAN types in the next chapter), but only if there are only two stations on any individual conversation and only as long as there aren't more than three or four simultaneous conversations on a single LAN. Anything beyond that will bring the network to its knees with startling quickness.

Until very recently, video conferencing wasn't even possible across the local area network. If you wanted *son et lumiere* (sound and light), you had to sign up for a high-speed digital phone line called Integrated Services Digital Network Primary Rate Interface, or ISDN-PRI, and your videoconferences were routed across these lines. An ISDN-PRI line is capable of carrying data at up to 1,544,000 bits per second, and you could expect to pay up to $1,500 per month just to have the line and several dollars a minute to actually use it.

The videoconferencing equipment was standalone, and cost from $5,000 for a very basic system to $50,000 to outfit a custom-designed conference room with multiple cameras and monitors.

That's no longer necessary. True, across-the-LAN videoconferencing is now available, on Ethernet or faster networks. A number of companies are offering point-to-point videoconferencing across local area networks, using both proprietary and standards-based hardware and software.

You need to realize one thing about LAN-based videoconferencing. It takes a lot of network capacity to move video or sound and video across the wire. All of the LAN-based systems use adaptive compression, which means that as long as there's plenty of bandwidth everything's going to be just fine. However, if someone down the hall starts a big database query that uses large portions of the network's capacity, the videoconferencing software is going to take a back seat.

The software will begin "dropping" frames from the video transmissions received if they arrive too late. This will show up as jerkiness on screen as the image "jumps" from one frame to another one that's actually a few frames later. The worse the bandwidth crunch, the more frames dropped and the jerkier the image. If you have hyperkinetic users who just naturally move around a lot, in a really bad capacity crunch it may appear to the person on the other end that you have perfected teleportation. Sound quality is going to remain consistent, though. The videoconferencing software reasons that it's more important to hear everything than it is to see everything, so sound transmission is prioritized.

The four major players in the LAN videoconferencing arena are C-Phone, VideoLabs, PictureTel, and Intel. Let's take a look at Intel's solution first.

Earlier, we said that there would be side benefits if you chose Intel's Indeo solution for video-enabled e-mail. ProShare LAN is that side benefit (Figure 2.4). You can add point-to-point LAN videoconferencing for the cost of the controlling software alone, currently around $1500 for a five-user system. That doesn't mean five users per conversation but rather up to four and a half

Figure 2.4 Intel's ProShare LAN workstation.

simultaneous conversations. Yes, that's right. Four and a half conversations, making Intel the perfect solution for people who want to talk to themselves.

Intel's ProShare camera sits on top of your video display, and to adjust the image you move the display itself. This solution doesn't take up any room on the desktop, but is somewhat limited in flexibility. You can also mount the camera on a mini-tripod that sits on your desk.

The system uses the Indeo compression methodology and provides windows on screen that are about ¼ the size of the overall screen on a Super VGA monitor. Quality is very good, especially when you consider that the "cost per seat" for full LAN videoconferencing with sound and video-enabled e-mail is less than $2,000.

The second largest competitor in LAN videoconferencing is VideoLabs. This company has an innovative camera design with a very small camera lens mounted on a gooseneck stalk that can be positioned any way that you like for a comfortable viewing environment. There's even a version of the camera that installs into an unused hard or floppy disk bay in the computer, with the gooseneck sticking out of the middle!

When it comes time to move images across the LAN the Videolabs FlexCam (Figure 2.5) uses the H.320 international standard for videoconferencing and packages the video inside whatever protocol your network uses. This takes up a little more bandwidth than the other companies' solutions, but does provide compatibility with dial-up external videoconferencing so that you can talk to people outside the company (with the appropriate type of line and dialing hardware).

The real up-and-comer in videoconferencing is Target Technologies and its C-Phone system (Figure 2.6). This company is doing some very innovative things with regard to the design and implemention of its systems.

First, C-Phone views the videoconferencing system as analogous to your telephone system. Videoconferences are initiated like phone calls, and the

Figure 2.5 VideoLabs' FlexCam.

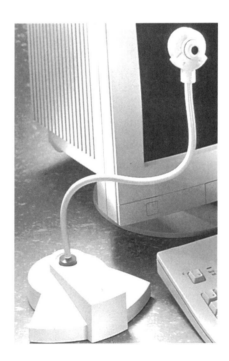

Figure 2.6 Target Technologies' C-Phone.

same types of services that your office phone offers, such as hold, Call Waiting, Caller ID, and even answering machine capabilities, are all replicated in C-Phone's controlling software.

The C-Phone system uses a proprietary compression and transmission method across local area networks. Target Technologies claims that its method has no effect on network bandwidth and that you can have up to 32 simultaneous "calls" active at once on an Ethernet network (this claim has not been verified, and the company's documentation offers no details to back it up). Multipoint videoconferencing is supported as the video equivalent of a telephone conference call.

There are several other features that make C-Phone a strong contender in the videoconferencing arena. If you want to attach two local area networks to make a wide area network and support videoconferencing across the link, C-Phone will let you do it but in a totally different way from what you might expect.

To call a user on another LAN, C-Phone takes the proprietary transmission method and converts it to the H.320 international videoconferencing standard. Instead of having to add an H.320 conversion board to each personal computer, you install a "video server" with one or more H.320 Coder/Decoder (CODEC) boards. These boards are available in a pool on a first come, first-served basis. The CODEC boards can talk across a dedicated wide area link or across dial-up digital lines to any other H.320-compatible system.

Because H.320 capability is pooled, the incremental cost of adding this capability can be as low as $500 per station, depending on the number of stations and the number of CODECs. This compares very favorably against the usual $2,000 per station for dedicated H.320 capability.

C-Phone also supports several other standards. Audio is transmitted using the G.711, G.722 or G.728 standards and C-Phone claims to be the first manufacturer to support the new T.120 international standard for integrating whiteboarding applications with videoconferences. As more manufacturers implement this standard it will mean better interoperability with videoconferencing systems at other companies in other places.

The new kid on the block when it comes to LAN videoconferencing is PictureTel, even though PictureTel is one of the oldest videoconferencing companies around. In the past PictureTel concentrated dedicated systems for dial-up videoconferencing and they were very good at it. PictureTel systems are commonly acknowledged as the best available for external videoconferencing systems, and are priced accordingly.

Several years ago PictureTel introduced "low-end" systems for external teleconferencing using the desktop PC as the base hardware instead of their own excellent (and expensive) systems. The PCS 100 and PCS 50 are both solid solutions for external teleconferencing using H.320 and ISDN telephone lines. Last year they decided they wanted "in" to the LAN marketplace as well and brought out the LiveLAN/V system (Figure 2.7).

The LiveLAN/V system comes with one of PictureTel's excellent entry level video cameras, Logitech's MovieMan full duplex audio and video capture

Figure 2.7 The PictureTel LIveLAN/V.

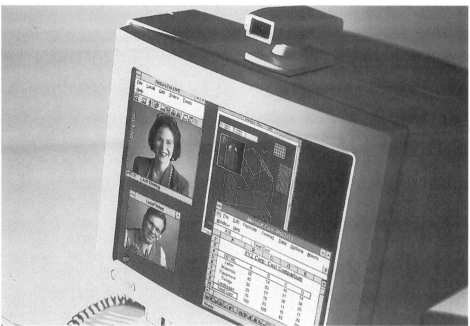

board, and all the cables you need to hook it all up. It also includes the video controller software and a very good whiteboarding program.

As with other manufacturers' products LiveLAN/V uses a proprietary compression method to keep transmission lean across the network. One notable feature of the LiveLAN system is that it watches overall network traffic and automatically scales the video frame rate back when things get busy, then brings it up again when they quiet down. LiveLAN/V works across Novell IPX/SPX networks or TCP/IP, but only when you use FTP Software's OnNet TCP/IP protocol software. They'll also support Windows 95 when the Winsock 2.0 specification is ready in early 1996.

There's also a gateway that contains one network interface and one ISDN Basic Rate Interface (BRI) adapter. This turns the proprietary video information into H.320 for transmission across digital dial-up circuits.

There's one more thing that you'll need if you go with PictureTel, and this bears a bit of explanation: PictureTel's system requires that you install their LiveManager software onto a Novell server if you're running IPX/SPX or a Windows NT server if you're using TCP/IP. You only have to purchase and install one LiveManager for the whole network, but you do have to have it present. LiveManager is controlled from any computer running Microsoft Windows attached to that server.

Why did they do this? The are a couple of very good reasons and it's likely that you'll see other manufacturers follow their lead in the not too distant future.

By now you've noticed that each of the companies we've discussed uses either their own proprietary method for moving video across the LAN (or MPEG or H.320, neither of which were designed for that kind of use). In order to communicate across a WAN or by dial-up the system has to translate to H.320, and there's no standard way of translating everything, including voice, video and whiteboarding sessions.

In order to correct this there's a new standard coming for LAN videoconferencing including gateways, or the boxes that turn proprietary into open and then shoot it out into the world. The standard will be called H.323, and as the number suggests, it's an extension of the H.320 standard.

The H.323 standard follows a client/server model and requires three separate components: the desktop (client), the gateway (server), and a gatekeeper or conference manager (The LiveManager software) that keeps track of the individual connections, makes sure that not to many simultaneous conversations are going on, and also provides video "phone books" and "Caller ID" type features. The standard should be completed and ratified by mid-1996.

PictureTel is very active on the committees that formulate industry standards, so they've decided to build their systems in such a way that they'll support these standards easily when the standards are released.

Even with these extra pieces, the LiveLAN system is surprisingly affordable, especially when you consider that it's PictureTel we're talking about. Each workstation costs $1,195 and includes the camera, capture board, a set of speakers (you might want to toss in a few bucks for headphones) and a microphone. The LiveManager software is $595, and there's no additional hardware required at the server to support it.

Some Interesting Hybrids

One of the most challenging aspects of deciding which videoconferencing standard to select (and one of the most challenging aspects of writing about them) is the fact that the industry is still very new. Things are in a constant state of flux, with new technologies being developed almost daily.

Each company in this field takes a slightly different tack towards achieving the goal of getting people to look at each other using their computers in real time. The four companies we've discussed so far use basically the same approach and differ materially only in which compression standard they have selected.

There are other ways to go about it, and two companies have definitely gone their own way. Viewpoint Systems, Inc., has come up with Personal Viewpoint, a hardware and software combination that allows you have true multipoint videoconferencing across an Ethernet LAN without affecting network traffic materially. The company claims that you can select the amount of network bandwidth used in a range from 56K to 640K bits per second.

Personal Viewpoint costs less than $2,000 per workstation, and that includes the software, a CODEC and video capture board, and a color camera. The software that controls it all is sophisticated and comprehensive, and includes call management features and built-in whiteboarding!

That's the good news. The bad news is that in order to achieve both high efficiency and low cost, Viewpoint Systems had to leave a few things out and make some design decisions that might be problematic.

The major item left out is sound. Personal Viewpoint is a *video-only* video-conferencing system. If you want to actually talk to the people you're looking at you'll have to have a telephone handy; and if the conference is multipoint, you'll need to make it a conference call. If you're operating across a wide area network, this can run up your cost of operations quite a bit.

Another potential difficulty is that Personal Viewpoint uses its own CODEC with a patented, proprietary compression method called Compressed Packet Video (CPV). If you choose this product, interoperability will be a problem, but you won't be alone there. Take a look at the next section for details.

The last item of interest about this product has to do with a design decision the company made. Personal Viewpoint uses the TCP/IP network protocol to communicate across the LAN. We'll talk about network protocols in detail later in this chapter, but the odds are about 3 to 1 that your network is not using this protocol now. That means added complexity in the installation and possible adverse effects on the rest of your networked applications.

Even with these potential limitations Personal Viewpoint may be right for your organization. If you're not going to use video-enabled electronic mail (remember that Personal Viewpoint uses a proprietary compression method and can't capture or store sound) or try to communicate across a wide area network regularly (think of the cost of all those long-distance conference calls), then the very low cost of this system may appeal to you.

The other company falling into the "very interesting" category is Incite Corporation. What these guys have done is exciting, innovative, and incredibly expensive, but it works.

All local area networks operate on an asynchronous basis. That means that when they need to send data they send it along with headers and checksums that ensure that the data gets to its destination intact. Timing isn't an issue because the data carries its own timing. This works great for transmission of pure data because you never know when a workstation will need something. If multiple workstations have traffic, that traffic is sequenced together on a space-available basis.

Video information doesn't work that way. Once a connection is established, you expect to send an uninterrupted flow of data (the constantly changing video image) until the conversation is completed. To do it right, you apply timing externally to save bandwidth. That's called isochronous data transmission.

There is a little-known standard for Metropolitan Area Networks (MANs) called IEEE 802.9a that makes use of isochronous transmission and attaches standard twisted-pair Ethernet as well. What you end up with is 10 megabits per second of data capability and 6.144 megabits per second of isochronous voice and video as well.

Incite manufactures a line of software and devices it calls isoEthernet. There are special cards for the personal computer, hubs, and wide area networking routers that all support this hybrid capability. Regular data flows on the 10 Mbps Ethernet side, and you get to choose what kind of video to support: MPEG or H.320. Voice and video flow on the 6.144 Mbps side. With that kind of bandwidth you can support any networked multimedia application you choose. (See Figure 2.8.)

Figure 2.8 Incite's Multimedia Hub.

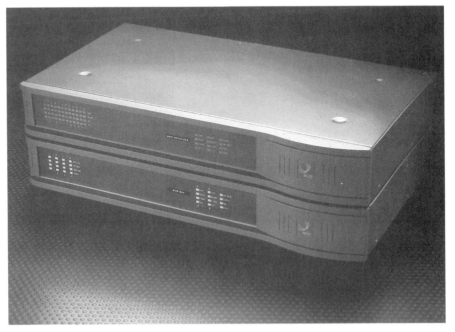

It sounds too good to be true, but it really is almost perfect. The not so perfect part is the cost. This technology requires special isoEthernet cards in each workstation ($300 each), Incite's Multimedia Hub ($5,500 for a 12- port hub) and a special Multimedia Manager server running Windows NT and Incite's software ($100 per user).

If you total it all up, you find that you're looking at around $1,000 per workstation, including a portion of the cost of the server. If you select H.320 video, add $2,500 per computer for the card and camera, and if you pick MPEG, add $1,900 per computer. This is one hellaciously expensive solution to the bandwidth crunch.

If you're building the brand-new LAN of your dreams, this might be the ticket for you. Those of us who have to live on normal-sized budgets will only stare enviously through the windows as you spend huge dollars on a terrific collaborative computing solution.

I Have H.320; You Have MPEG. Houston, We Have a Problem Here.

Interconnectivity is indeed a potential problem. It's only potential right now because there are currently very few companies actually using videoconferencing, and of those even fewer are talking to each other. The bare fact of the matter is that every single one of the encoding methods used for videoconferencing is totally incompatible with every other method.

Videoconferencing hardware and software need to use compression to move images across LANs and other circuits. There's only so much bandwidth available, and without compression videoconferencing would take it all and still need more. Even a video "window" comprises hundreds of thousands of bits of data, and full-motion video uses 30 frames per second, running the raw data requirement up into the millions-of-bits-per-second range.

Data compression is what makes video across digital circuits possible, and the compression methods in current use are extremely efficient. The H.320 standard provides compression ratios that are typically around 20:1, or 1 bit of transmitted data for every 20 bits of raw data. Indeo and QuickTime are both slightly less efficient than H.320, and MPEG is slightly more efficient.

What prompts a manufacturer to choose one method over another is most often the cost of the circuits used to compress and decompress data rather than relative efficiencies. It should be no surprise that Intel chose Indeo, which was its own standard using its own hardware, and Apple chose QuickTime, which is also Apple proprietary. H.320 and MPEG are both true industry standards, blessed by their respective sanctioning organizations.

Because all of these methods require specific hardware to perform the actual compression/decompression operation, there aren't any manufacturers that support multiple compression types. You pays your money and you takes your method.

If you and the person you want to talk to are both using the same method, there's no problem, even if the manufacturers of your respective videoconferencing equipment are different. The standards themselves are well defined, so H.320 talks to H.320, Indeo talks to Indeo, and so forth.

But what if you want to make H.320 talk to Indeo? The simple answer is that you can't, but someone else can. What it will take is the services of an intermediary that will accept the signals from each participant and convert them into the signals that the other participants use.

Right now you can buy this conversion service on a per-minute basis from Sprint, AT&T, and Wiltel. MCI has also announced a videoconferencing center, but has not yet made it available to the general public. Oh yeah, it's expensive. The last published numbers were around $2 per minute per participant, which is understandable when you consider that the equipment necessary to convert the format costs a cool million dollars for each installation.

The only reasonable alternative is to purchase more than one type of videoconferencing installation with the full knowledge that they aren't interoperable and that the only thing you'll use them for is to talk to people at other locations with the same type of setup. This is prohibitively expensive for small companies, so it's really not much of a solution.

ALMOST BUT NOT QUITE MULTIMEDIA: STATIC IMAGES

Many businesses have very heavy paper requirements. Doctor's offices and insurance companies are excellent examples of workplaces that are positively awash in forms that are either generated by computer or contain information that needs to be entered into the computer.

Let this go on long enough and your company can drown in all those forms. File folders go into file cabinets. File cabinets go into file storage rooms. File storage rooms go into file storage facilities, and pretty soon the purpose of the business becomes document storage and retrieval regardless of what you started out doing.

Your company might have a need to store pictures rather than images, or even compound documents with both pictures and text in them. Real estate agencies often have large "books" of home and commercial listings, with pages describing the building or house accompanied by one or more photographs. This system works okay until you have more than one person who needs to look at the "book" at the same time. The conventional solution would be to make more "books" with more paper and more photographs. There's got to be a better way, and there is.

Electronic Document Storage and Retrieval

How can you reverse this tide of paperwork? One way is to take all those documents and store them electronically using the computer, some specialized hardware, and document management software.

Document images are both the easiest and most difficult to store and retrieve across the network. They're easy because the technology to capture and store them is a mature one—the scanner. They're hard because once stored, they no longer make any sense. That nice, legible form with its neatly ordered rows and columns of information is now just as mass of ones and zeros stored in a graphics file. It can't be extracted, sorted, tabulated, or manipulated without some extraordinary action.

What you'll need is document management software, and an excellent example is Pagekeeper, from Caere Corporation. The secret behind this program and any other document management program is Optical Character Recognition (OCR). As the document is scanned, the program looks at it and translates it into both a text file and a graphics file. The text part is stored either in the graphics file or in a separate database, and you can perform keyword searches and other operations on the text in order to find the image you want.

The image part of the file needs some attention, too. When first scanned, it's huge! Simple math tells us that an 8½-by-11 inch piece of paper scanned at 300 dots per inch is going to result in a raw file of 8,415,000 pixels, or an easy megabyte of disk space per document. Obviously, we can't allow this to happen, especially since most documents are 80 percent white space, devoid of information.

So, the next step is for the document management software to compress the image and eliminate all the extra information and white space. When this is done, the image will be about one-tenth of its former size or less, and will be stored in a graphics image format. Usually, that format is going to be either PCX or GIF. You'll be interested to know that the PCX format is the same one that your Fax machine uses "on the fly" to send facsimiles across the phone lines. If the document has multiple pages, it'll be stored as a DCX file, but the method is the same.

Graphics Image Format (GIF) files are stored differently, but the end result is the same. GIF files are the most common interchange format across the Internet, so with the "Information Superhighway" gaining speed this file type is picking up a lot of converts.

Later you're going to want to call the document back up and view or print it. The document management program takes care of that, too. Remember the text file? The program probably did a keyword extraction that allows you to locate, retrieve, and view the file in short order. Printing it out again is just a matter of pressing a few keys, but remember that the entire file, all 8 million pixels or so, has to be translated into printerspeak and sent to that laser printer. This is going to have a definite impact on your network if the printer is shared, and the printer itself may need a memory upgrade to be capable of handling that large a graphical image.

There are a couple of ways to deal with this bandwidth crunch. Using one or more dedicated printers is one way, albeit a rather expensive one. Another way is to equip the printer and its controlling PC with an image processing board combo. This hardware-based solution compresses the print image within the PC and sends the compressed bitstream to a matching board in the printer, which decompresses it and then hands it off to the printer controller. Since all of this happens within the printer instead of across the network, greatly improved speed results and less network bandwidth is required.

That's document storage in a nutshell. Obviously, this is a very visual environment, so all of the currently popular document management programs are Microsoft Windows based.

A Picture Is Worth 10,847 Bytes (or Thereabouts)

There is a lot of interest in storage of photographic and drawn images these days, particularly as components of databases. Why include a written description of a house when you can show that house to a prospective buyer in the comfort of your own office? Why simply list the number of rooms and their sizes when you can call up the floor plan with a few keystrokes?

Earlier, we discussed PCX and GIF image storage. Both of these formats can be used for photographs as well as documents, and both are known as "lossless." In other words, the compression algorithms used work in the exact opposite way when you want to view the image later, and the image appears exactly as it did when first compressed. Some photographic images really don't need that level of control. It's acceptable to lose some color or resolution information in order to achieve a smaller stored file size. That's where JPEG comes in. Named after the Joint Photographic Experts Group that created the standard, JPEG is a "lossy" standard for storing and retrieving visual images. (See Figure 2.9.)

GIF and PCX are more efficient when it comes to images that have very few colors or a lot of white space, such as line drawings or even cartoons. JPEG

Figure 2.9 16.7 million color JPEG image (left), 256 color bitmap image (middle), and 16 color PCX image (right).

really excels at photographic or photorealistic images, so all three standards have their place.

When a photograph is scanned each individual pixel up to the resolution of the scanner (usually up to 600 dots per inch) is scanned along with that pixel's color value. The color value can be recorded as CMYK (Cyan, Magenta, Yellow in Kelvins), RGBI (Red, Green, Blue Information), or HSV (Hue, Saturation, Value), depending on the scanner software. JPEG is a software-only compression method, and the speed of compression and decompression is directly related to the speed of the processor. An older 386SX-based computer is probably going to be unacceptably slow at retrieving and displaying JPEG images.

In order to store the data JPEG looks at adjacent pixels and records not their actual values but the differences between their values. If you expand the image on screen, the individual pixels get larger and some of the color information get thrown out. When you shrink the image again, that information cannot be recaptured and the resolution of the image suffers. Why would we do this? Because JPEG is an extremely efficient storage format. An image that would be 200,000 bytes as a GIF would be less than 30,000 bytes as a JPEG.

Because of the compression methods available, image storage has very little effect on the network. Images are stored as very tightly compacted bundles of bits, and retrieving them uses no more bandwidth than the equivalent amount of textual information.

The effect on individual computers is another matter entirely. The station you use to scan and compress images should be a late-model 486 or top-of-the-line Macintosh with a large local hard drive for the compression process. The station used to decompress and display photographic or drawn images should have at least a late-model 80386DX processor (or be a late-model Macintosh) and, more important, be capable of displaying at least 800 × 600 pixels in 256 colors. Early VGA monitors aren't going to meet this standard, and you may be looking at some video upgrades to keep your users happy.

AND IN THE MIDDLE . . . THE NETWORK OPERATING SYSTEM

Despite all of the components necessary to support networked multimedia, you may be surprised to learn that the network operating system isn't likely to change much, if at all.

Think of the Network Operating System (NOS) as an enabler for all the other components. It acts as a repository of information, but the nature of that information is unimportant to it. It also acts as a postal clerk, accepting and delivering the mail, but it never reads the letters that it carries.

Since NOSs are just middlemen as far as multimedia is concerned, there usually isn't anything that you need to do to the software to make the sounds and pictures flow. However, for most NOSs there are configuration options that you need to be aware of and allow for if multimedia applications are to flow unimpeded.

Parts of the Network Operating System

Network operating systems are essentially divided into three components: Core services, which are the actions that allow the server to manage itself, User services, like storing and retrieving files across the network, and Directory services, which allow the server to manage user access. (See Figure 2.10.)

Core services are the internal functions that the server performs to keep itself going, such as deciding how much processor time to allocate to file storage and retrieval functions, network packet routing, and the like. Core services don't actually do these things because that's the user services function. All they do is divide up the total amount of processor resources and parcel them out. Some NOSs allow you to run programs on the server itself, and in this case Core services are also responsible for allocating time to the programs and making sure that they don't interfere with each other.

Figure 2.10 Parts of the network operating system.

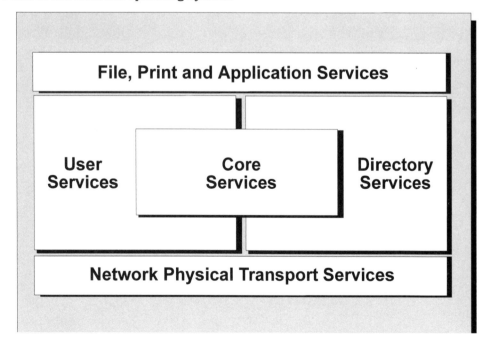

File, Print and Application Services

User Services   **Core Services**   **Directory Services**

Network Physical Transport Services

The User services function is where most of the work gets done as far as you and I are concerned. User services are responsible for the actual process of accepting data for storage and retrieving it upon request, routing data to the appropriate network adapter for delivery across the network, and gathering, scheduling, and delivering print jobs. It's not glamorous, but it's absolutely necessary.

The most important function that the NOS performs is Directory services. The term *Directory*, as used here, refers to people, not files. In simple terms this is the list of people who are allowed to use the network, what parts of the network they are allowed to use, and any restrictions on how they use it. Different network types use different terminology, but the function remains the same regardless of the vendor.

Getting from Here to There: Transport Protocols

Underlying all of this is the transport protocol. This is the packaging that servers and workstations fit data into before shipping it across the network. Some transport protocols are simple and efficient; others are complicated and ungainly. Often you can pick which protocols you want to use with an operating system as a separate decision at installation time. There are three major protocol sets in use these days: IPX, TCP/IP, and NetBIOS/NetBEUI. Each has its advantages and disadvantages, especially when it comes to transporting multimedia information.

IPX is less than ideal for multimedia because for every packet of information sent across the wire, a return packet acknowledging receipt must be sent. This obviously uses bandwidth that could be better employed elsewhere. There is a way around this problem, but it's only available on "pure" Novell networks. If that's your playground, take a look at the NetWare section below.

For all of this, IPX is a very efficient protocol. There isn't a lot of other overhead associated with its use, such as longer addresses that plump up the packets or the redundant signaling that other protocols use.

The most popular "other" protocol is Transmission Control Protocol/ Internet Protocol (TCP/IP), which, as its name suggests, is the basic protocol used on the Internet. TCP/IP is actually a suite of individual protocols, each of which has its own specialty, like File Transfer Package (FTP) and Network File System (NFS). Because the protocol suite is modular, it is usually pretty efficient, but it does have one major problem when applied to multimedia.

TCP/IP was designed for the Internet, a giant conglomeration of computers all coupled loosely (sometimes very loosely) together, so it makes the basic assumption that communications between computers will be unreliable and, under most circumstances, never checks to make sure that a packet actually makes it to its destination. If you're moving a file from one place to another, it's pretty easy for a program to see that there's a chunk missing and request that it be resent, but what about real-time audio or video? What happens is that the data feed starts to get jumpy as packets are lost or corrupted en route and those packets are simply lost. In a videoconference someone might seem to teleport across the room, or the audio portion will get crackly or break up altogether. This is less than desirable.

If you're communicating across a public internetwork, like the Internet, transmission delays as thousands upon thousands of other people try to move their data at the same time are also common, with a less than desirable effect on the quality of transmission.

Despite all these shortcomings, both IPX and TCP/IP are better networking protocols than the third option, the Network Basic Input Output System (NetBIOS)/Network BIOS Enhanced User Interface (NetBEUI), which suffers from extreme protocol bloat.

NetBIOS/NetBEUI is a very old protocol set. It was designed for the original IBM personal computer and IBM's PC LAN operating system. PC LAN is a peer-to-peer system that assumes that any computer on the LAN must be capable of both being a client and using resources on other computers, and being a server that makes resources available to other computers. In order to accomplish this IBM shoehorned everything but the kitchen sink into the NetBIOS/NetBEUI, which adds an additional 30 percent or so to the data stream just for overhead and control messages.

In order to process the control messages NetBIOS/NetBEUI takes a fair amount of the computer's processing capability. In fact, it takes so much of it that it's entirely unsuitable for any kind of networked multimedia application. What happens is that when a packet arrives, the receiver takes so long to open and authenticate it that the interval for the packet to be acknowledged "times out" and the sender automatically resends it. After that the sender gets an acknowledgment of the first packet, sends the second packet, gets a *second* acknowledgment of the first packet when it is waiting for an acknowledgment of the second packet, it throws its metaphorical hands up in disgust and starts the whole process over again.

Now that we have a general idea of what the NOS does and how it gets the word out to users, let's take a look at the major network operating systems in use and how they stack up, multimedia-wise.

Novell NetWare

The most popular NOS is Novell Corporation's NetWare. Around 60 percent of all the networks in the world are built around various versions of NetWare running on dedicated file servers with Intel microprocessors. There are currently two popular versions of NetWare, 3.12 and 4.10. The earlier version is typically used for local area networks with less than 10 servers, and the later version is used for enterprise networks with 10 or more servers.

On 3.12, Directory services are provided in a set of three files called the Binderies, and each server gets its own set. If you have one or more users who have to be able to use multiple servers, you must add them to the Binderies of each server separately, which is a pain. Version 4.10 takes care of this by keeping Directory services in a global file called NetWare Directory Services (NDS), which is replicated to each server on the network simultaneously. NDS is so useful on large networks that it's the single largest reason that people choose to upgrade from 3.12

Since they invented it, NetWare uses IPX as the basic transport protocol, but it can be modified to use other protocols as well. The IPX process of acknowledging every packet sent can be a real drag on multimedia applications, so you have two choices for getting around the problem. The first is an add-in to the NetWare environment called "Packet Burst" that allows a server or workstation to gather up a sequence of packets, send them all together, and then wait for a single acknowledgment packet in return.

Packet Burst has both good and bad points: On the good side, the number of acknowledgment (ACK) packets is minimized. On the not so good side, allowing individual workstations to tie up the network cable for the longer time it takes to send a group of packets can make the network kind of jumpy for other workstations.

The other alternative is to use another protocol, such as TCP/IP.

So what's the best choice for multimedia on NetWare? It depends on how you plan to use the network. If you're only going to be doing multimedia on your own network, choose IPX with Packet Burst. If you're going to connect to other, possibly non-NetWare networks (like the Internet), then choose TCP/IP.

Microsoft LAN Manager/IBM LAN Server

The second most popular NOS is Microsoft's LAN Manager (that's what it used to be called)/LAN Server (that's what it's called now). While NetWare uses a dedicated server to provide Core, User, and Directory services, LAN Manager can be run in either dedicated or nondedicated mode on a computer with Microsoft's Windows NT operating system, and IBM's LAN Server runs under the OS/2 operating system. Since both programs come from a common heritage back in the days when Microsoft and IBM were still talking to each other, we can talk about them both together.

One nice thing about LAN Manager/LAN Server is that it's modular. You can install the entire package to create a true network server, or just the portions that allow a computer to function as a file, print, or communications server.

Another asset of this NOS is that it's simple to install and administer. While NetWare is complex enough that Novell has a training and certification program for administrators, LAN Server can be administered by a moderately smart, moderately technical person with no specific training. LAN Server's greatest liability is that Directory services are still specific to each server. There are no global directories available, so you have to plug each user into each server that they'll need access to. Microsoft has promised global directories in the next version of the NOS, but it's not available yet.

LAN Server has two "native" transport protocols, NetBIOS/NetBEUI and TCP/IP. When you install the NOS, you can specify either or both of them. If you're going to enter the world of networked multimedia, TCP/IP is your best (and really only) choice.

Banyan VINES

Think of it as computer evolution. When Banyan Systems, Inc. introduced VINES, the server was loosely based on the UNIX operating system and the network was of the company's own construction. As time passed and successive versions were introduced, VINES became more purely UNIX-like—so much so that the current version is virtually indistinguishable from a mature UNIX with networking features.

Directory services are provided by Banyan's enhancement to UNIX Directories, called StreetTalk, which provides global Directories. In fact, Banyan was the first company to offer global Directories.

VINES has a tendency to be a very polarizing NOS. There are many people who use it and are fanatical about it, disparaging other NOSs as "toys" and "playthings." People who don't use VINES are put off by this attitude and have a tendency to discount its value as "geekware." The reality is that VINES is a very powerful NOS that shows its stuff on really, really big networks that typically have hundreds or even thousands of workstations.

The native transport protocol is TCP/IP, and it is very difficult to induce VINES to support other protocols. This makes it a pretty good choice for multimedia, with fast, powerful server software and an acceptable transport layer.

Microsoft Windows and Windows NT

The good news is that when you bought Microsoft Windows for Workgroups, Windows 95, or Windows NT, you bought a capable peer-to-peer operating system that allows you to communicate, share files and printers, and send electronic mail. The bad news is that if you leave it in the default configuration, you're using NetBIOS/NetBEUI and it's incredibly slow and ungainly.

The Microsoft Network is a simplified NOS that allows any computer on the network to publish resources, such as hard drives or even individual directories on those hard drives, as available to other users for reading or modifying. Printers can also be shared in this manner.

Regrettably, there is no such thing as global Directory service on the Microsoft Network. Because every computer can act as a server, you have to establish user access rights on each server independently.

For multimedia applications the Microsoft Network is going to be less than desirable, because of the load that making the computer act as both a server and a workstation imposes, and because of the inherently slow nature of NetBIOS/NetBEUI. You can help things along by not making individual workstations assume server tasks unless they absolutely have to, and by specifying an alternative protocol like TCP/IP at installation time. Even if you do both of these, though, be aware that it may not be enough.

Lantastic

Lantastic is another peer-to-peer operating system from Artisoft that allows all computers on the network to be servers, clients, or both. Depending on the version that you buy, the transport protocol will be either Artisoft's own slimmed-down version of NetBIOS/NetBEUI (Lantastic 6.0, Lantastic for OS/2) or IPX (Lantastic for NetWare). Optionally, you can install TCP/IP support as well.

Because it's a mature operating system (after all, you don't get to version 6.0 without going through a lot of changes along the way), Lantastic is a fairly speedy NOS that doesn't take up a lot of memory in the computer or demand too much processor time. Even so, you'll really need to pay attention to the speed and age of the computer you're running it on, and you may very well find that even late-generation 486 PCs just don't have the horsepower to do networked multimedia *and* be file servers on the network at the same time.

Lantastic also does not offer global Directory services. Each server must be configured individually with user names and access rights. As long as the network stays small that's not too much of a problem, but if your network has 50 or more users and highly distributed data sets you might want to consider reorganizing things.

Networking with UNIX

UNIX has been around for a long time. Invented at AT&T Bell Labs, it was made available free to colleges and universities, which definitely helped its acceptance in the marketplace as all those users graduated and went out into the real world.

Networking has always been an integral part of the UNIX operating system. TCP/IP was originally developed to tie all those university computers together across a network called ARPAnet (Advanced Research Projects Administration), based on UNIX computers, that later evolved into the Internet. However, multimedia has not been integral to UNIX until recently.

Most early UNIX-based computers were minicomputers that serviced anywhere from a few to a few hundred users on dumb terminals that were entirely character-based. They had no graphics, no color, no sound—not much of anything except screens of text, but X11 changed all that. The X Windows system for UNIX (not to be confused with Microsoft Windows, which is a completely different thing) allows workstations with their own processors and RAM to communicate graphically with UNIX servers, or UNIX computers with the appropriate hardware to act as both servers and X Windows workstations. Computers manufactured by Sun Computer, Inc., and Silicon Graphics, Inc., are excellent examples of this breed.

These late-generation workstations have support for CD-ROM, audio, and real-time video. In fact, most of them are significantly *more* capable of networked multimedia than Intel-based PCs, by virtue of the fact that they are several times more powerful than their PC cousins. However, before you run out and buy them you should be aware that while they're more powerful, they're also more expensive, at two to three times the cost of a modern desktop personal computer.

3 COMPONENTS OF NETWORKED MULTIMEDIA— HARDWARE

In this chapter we'll look at the bits and pieces necessary to construct or upgrade to a multimedia-capable network, starting at the desktop and working our way in to the server.

ON THE DESKTOP

The desktop computer can run the gamut from a slow, boring blob that simply gets the job done to a flashy piece of equipment with every conceivable piece of multimedia hardware installed. Let's take a look at the machine itself on a component-by-component basis, starting with the processor. In each of the following sections we'll examine IBM personal computers based on Intel and compatible microprocessors first, and then we'll talk a little bit about Apple computers with Motorola processors (both the older 68000 and newer PowerPC types).

If your network is like most, you still have a few microcomputers based on the Intel 80286 processor. Flush 'em. They're not going to do you any good at all as workstations for the simple reason that they can't run Microsoft Windows in 386 Enhanced mode, which most multimedia software requires. Make them into print servers or flower boxes, because that's about all they're going to be good for.

If you have 80386SX-based computers, you have a beginning multimedia station. About all you're going to be able to do with them, though, is white-boards and sound-enabled e-mail and none of the fancier stuff. You can extend their lifetimes by adding a math coprocessor and making sure that they have eight megabytes of RAM, and if you have a 20-megahertz or faster processor, you can look into a processor upgrade from AMD or Cyrix, turning the computer into a pseudo-486. Likewise for the 80386DX. These computers can be upgraded to sort-of 486s to very good effect for just a little cash.

The Intel 486 is the real starting point for true networked multimedia. This means the 486DX, by the way, not the 486SX. The SX chip is basically just a fast 80386, and you need the math coprocessor and cache RAM that is built into the DX for complete effectiveness. If you have one of the newer DX2 or DX4 variants, you're really doing well and should have no problem adding any multimedia except multipoint videoconferencing.

If you have a Pentium processor, you're doing fine. Even the original 60-megahertz version has more than enough power to tackle any networked multimedia application.

Mac users take note: If your Mac is over two years old, you've got problems. Apple really started to get things right with the introduction of the Quadra series, and, of course, the PowerMac is the ultimate in Apples. Anything older than these is severely limited in both processing power and expansion capability, and you're going to have difficulty adding new technologies to old boxes.

Some More RAM, Please, Ma'am

How much memory are you going to need? A lot. No, strike that. More. No wait, that's still not enough. Get the idea? It used to be that two megabytes of RAM was considered the "normal" amount, and four megabytes was optimal. As applications and environments continue to grow in size, four is minimum and eight is considered the right number today. There seems to be a "sweet spot," to use the tennis term, in the Windows environment at 8 MB.

Be prepared to increase that. It seems likely that the operating systems of the future, including OS/2 Warp and its next incarnation and Windows 95, will consider eight megabytes of RAM to be a practical minimum and 16 will be the desired number. This can add up to some serious money if RAM prices stay at current levels. (In early 1995 RAM cost about $40 per megabyte and had been at this level for about a year.)

Over in Apple land, you're already aware that Macs eat RAM like candy. 12 MB is the minimum these days, 24 MB is good, and 32 is ideal.

Hard Drives

As applications programs increase in size, their storage requirements increase as well. You have two choices about where to put the programs and data: on a server or at the individual workstation. Both have their benefits and liabilities, but we need to take a couple of things into consideration.

One argument for putting programs and such on the server is that it's going to be a lot easier to manage them when they're all in one place. You can perform upgrades and fixes on a single computer, and everyone sees the results immediately. This is a powerful argument for centralization.

However, we're going to be using applications that are already extremely network intensive on the data side. If we load the applications on the server, then loading programs and overlays and storing and retrieving temporary files may push the network over the edge. Unless you have a really small network or a really fast one, it's usually better to put the applications and operating environment at the workstation despite the increased workload come upgrade time.

A number of software publishers are aware of this difficulty and are on the verge of releasing software distribution and management programs that will still allow you to do upgrades and fixes once only. Microsoft's Hermes system has gotten good prerelease reviews, as have several others. As a result, putting everything at the workstation may not stay a bad thing for long.

There's one other reason to think carefully before committing to local hard-drive installation of programs. You may be asking for trouble of a different sort. Let's say that you have decided to place operating copies of the software on hard drives in each of the computers that will need this application. You've done a careful study of how many people in the company will use this software and even figured out how many of those people will be using it at any given time. Under the "simultaneous use" provisions of your network license, that's how many copies you need to purchase, right?

Wrong. You're now running these applications on a single-user computer, and regardless of how many people are using it at one time, you have to have one license for that application for each computer that it's installed on. This situation is expensive and irritating, but until major manufacturers start to release software distribution systems that take local hard drive installation into account, you're going to be stuck with it.

CD-ROM Drives

Perhaps the most pressing issue facing network managers these is day is just exactly what to do about those pesky CD-ROM drives. As we discussed briefly in Chapter 1, more and more software publishers are presenting their wares in CD-ROM format rather than on the traditional floppy disks.

CD-ROM discs use the same technology as audio compact discs (CDs) do, storing information in a digital format as a series of microscopic pits burned into the disk surface. These pits are "read" by a laser beam, which interprets the presence of a pit as a binary 1 and the absence as a binary 0, or a single binary digit (bit) of information. How many of these pits are there on a single CD-ROM? Over 5 billion, allowing each CD-ROM to store around 660 million characters of information.

CD-ROM drives come in a variety of speeds, but only one size. Since the format for both the physical media and the manner of storing information on CD-ROM drives is standardized (the standard is called ISO-9660), the only options that manufacturers have is how fast you can get the information off the media and into your computer's RAM.

The original CD-ROM drives read information at around 150,000 bits per second, with an average access time of almost one-half second! This made CD-ROM retrieval times only slightly faster than those of floppy disks. A few years ago NEC Technologies figured out how to design a drive that provides twice the access speed provided by the original design, which is quite a trick when you think about it. (See Figure 3.1.)

If all you're reading off the drive is pure data, like spreadsheets and such, then doubling the access speed is a good thing because the faster it gets into RAM, the faster you can manipulate it, and so on. But what if the data is visual or auditory? A leisurely tour of the Amazon basin in a canoe suddenly looks like a speedboat tour of Disneyland's Jungle Cruise, and sound is even worse. Picture an entire world made up of people who talk like Alvin and the Chipmunks. See what I mean?

Figure 3.1 NEC Quad Speed CD-ROM Drive. Photo courtesy of NEC Technologies, Inc.

What the NEC drives did (and now pretty much every manufacturer does) is look at the format of the data intelligently. If it's video or audio, the drive automatically "throttles back" to 150,000 bits per second. If it's pure data, full speed ahead!

Now that the sound barrier's been broken, you can buy double, triple, quadruple, and even sextuple (six times the speed of the original specification) CD-ROM drives.

CD-ROM distribution is attractive to publishers for several reasons: First, they can store a lot of information on a single device. As programs and databases grow ever larger, the publisher no longer has to worry about the time and expense of mastering tens or even hundreds of floppy disks and then preparing tens of thousands of them for distribution. An excellent example is the latest version of Microsoft's Office Professional Suite. If you buy the floppy version, upon opening the box you will discover 31 floppy disks ready for you to install. Think about the amount of time necessary to copy those floppies, package them, and stuff them in the box. They made that box pretty heavy, too, and shipping hundreds of thousands of copies of Office made the freight companies very happy.

The second reason, and probably the more important one, is that you and I can copy floppy disks very easily. Now, I would never use the word *piracy*, but somewhere, sometime, someone is singing "Yo Ho, Yo Ho, Its a Pirate's Life for Me," and the legitimate software publishers don't like it.

CD-ROMs aren't easy to copy. It takes some fairly sophisticated and expensive equipment to make the copy, and only the hardest-core professional pirates are going to expend the effort to do so. By distributing programs and data on CD-ROM, the publisher eliminates the "casual" copying that has been the bane of their existence for almost as long as the industry has been around.

As we discussed in Chapter 1, adding CD-ROM to every workstation on the network can be expensive and time-consuming, and can present more problems than it fixes. Before you start doling out drives to every user who wants/needs/desires one, take a look at the section "Shared CD-ROM Drives" later in this chapter.

Show Me!

The video controller is another critical item for multimedia. If you're going to use motion video, you're going to need an accelerated video controller card with at least 1 MB of its own video RAM capable of displaying 256 colors at 800 × 600 pixel resolution. Higher resolutions, like 1024 × 768, or more colors will bump the RAM requirement to 2 MB at least.

An accelerated card is a video adapter that has three features: It has its own graphics processor on the card itself that performs some software-type functions like moving the mouse cursor in hardware instead; it has Direct Memory Access (DMA) so that video data moves directly from system RAM out to the card without having to pass through the main processor first; and it is a bus master. A bus master can control the expansion bus directly without having to get the main processor's attention by generating an interrupt signal on the bus. This effectively makes your computer a multiprocessor, with the graphics processor and the main processor operating simultaneously and independently.

One thing you'll want to look at closely when selecting a video adapter is that funny edge connector that sticks out of the top of the board. It's called a "feature connector," and that's exactly what it's for—it adds features to your video display.

The feature connector won't always appear as an edge connector like the one on the bottom of the board. Sometimes all you'll see is a double row of pins sticking straight out somewhere near the top of the board. That's okay—both styles do the exact same thing. But what do they do?

The most common thing that feature connectors are used for is to "piggyback" the video signal. Another board is installed with a cable attaching it to your video adapter. This board can be used to capture video from an external source to be displayed on your monitor (this is called a genlock board), play back compressed video from a hard disk or CD-ROM (that's an MPEG board), or even show you live TV programs (a TV tuner board).

You really do need to be careful when you select the video adapters that you'll use to upgrade the network. Why? Because when the feature connector was designed, there weren't any uses for it, and some manufacturers cut corners by putting on feature connectors that either didn't work at all or didn't work right.

Since you'll be putting MPEG players, video capture boards, or CODECs in your computers sooner or later, it will behoove you to make sure that the feature connectors work properly on the brand that you select.

Waiting for the Bus

For networked multimedia this is probably the single most critical component of the host PC. The expansion bus is that row of slots at the back of the computer where you plug in cards that represent additional capabilities for the computer like video and network controllers. The most common type of expansion slot is called the Industry Standard Architecture (ISA) bus, and it is horribly slow. Even though a personal computer can be operating at speeds of 100 Mhz or higher, the ISA expansion bus is artificially limited to the measly speed of 8 Mhz. This is because the original IBM Personal Computer/AT used an 8-Mhz processor and had an 8-Mhz expansion bus.

In recent years manufacturers have taken several runs at the problem of increasing bus speed. IBM brought out the PS/2 series of microcomputers with a new expansion bus type called MicroChannel Architecture, or MCA. The Microchannel Architecture allows for transfers on and off the bus at speeds up to 32 Mhz, or four times the speed of the original ISA bus.

IBM-compatible manufacturers countered with the Enhanced Industry Standard Architecture, or EISA, which is good for up to 32 Mhz as well but also supports "burst mode" transfers at up to 40 Mhz. EISA was a very expensive add-on to the computer architecture and added up to $700 to the price of otherwise equivalent machines. EISA expansion adapters were similarly more expensive, which definitely limited EISA's popularity.

Then the industry association that controlled standards for video interfaces, the Video Equipment Standards Association (VESA), got into the act. They reasoned that instead of improving the existing bus or proposing an alternative, they would just as soon avoid the whole issue and hook their equipment directly to the processor and RAM on a "local" bus. The resulting standard was called VL-BUS and was blazingly fast compared to other methods.

VL-BUS attained instant popularity with everyone except Intel, which wasn't making any of the chips that allowed VL-BUS to happen. The folks at Intel decided that since it was their microprocessor that everyone wanted to hook up to, it stood to reason that they could create an even better local bus. The result was a bus called the Peripheral Component Interconnect (PCI).

In order to support full networked multimedia, one of the four fast bus structures (MCA, EISA, VL-BUS, and PCI) is needed. The old-style ISA bus can only move information into and out of RAM at the snail's pace of less than 10 megabytes per second, and in reality 8 megabytes per second is really pushing it.

Look at the math involved in moving video over the LAN, for example. If the average video window is 320×200 pixels in size and supports 256 colors on screen simultaneously, then each frame of video is 64,000 bytes uncompressed. There are 30 frames for each second of video, so one second of video is 1,920,000 bytes of data! Add another 8,000 bytes per second for audio information, and another 20 percent for network overhead and error checking, and the total is 3,856,000 bytes per second. Now, remember that teleconferencing is bidirectional, so we have to double the total. We'll apply compression and cut the total by 80 percent, but at the cost of some of the processor's capacity. Every second that a single two-way videoconference is in operation, around 1,524,400 bytes have to be cleared on and off the expansion bus! If you're using Ethernet or Token Ring, you've just used up most of the bandwidth available to you and reduced your processor's capability to multitask as well.

With this in mind, you can see that more than a couple of point-to-point videoconferences at one time on one network is tough, and multipoint videoconferencing is completely out of the question. There isn't enough room on the wire to support more than a few conversations at one time. If you wanted to have a videoconference with more than one other participant, the expansion bus could not handle the data that would need to flow from the decompression circuitry across to RAM and the video controller.

The next item to discuss is all the stuff that goes in the back of the computer: expansion cards. Let's count them off: video controller, sound board, MPEG player board, video capture board, network adapter. A fully multimedia-enabled personal computer is going to be a busy box indeed.

Sound Boards

The sound board is the simplest and least expensive of the possible additions to your system. An entry-level board will set you back less than $100, and even the absolute best is around $700 right now. In the corporate environment there are very few users who would benefit from having the best of the best, though. If you have a graphics department or a corporate communications group that produces multimedia presentations, they might be worthy beneficiaries, but everyone else can get along just fine with one of the $100 jobs.

There are cheaper 8-bit sound boards that sell for around $50. Try to avoid them if you can. These boards are manufactured very inexpensively and don't have a lot of resistance to electromagnetic interference. Putting a cheap board in a fast PC will cause a lot of hiss in recorded sound that actually comes from electric fields thrown off by the processor and RAM. Better-quality 16-bit or 32-bit boards have correspondingly better protection against this.

One minor benefit of sound boards is that, because of the comparatively small amounts of information that are passed onto and off of the board, you don't need a fancy expansion bus to support them. Almost all sound boards are plain old ISA design and work just fine. Even boards designed with sound processors that manipulate 32 bits of information at a time do so simply to improve the sound quality, not to speed up the processing of that sound. If they did all you'd have would be the highest-fidelity Alvin and the Chipmunks player in town.

If you purchase a sound board for your computer, it comes with the ability to capture Wave sounds via a microphone or direct connection and to play those sounds back. It also comes with the ability to play files stored in the MIDI format. How it plays those files depends on the type of board, as does the cost.

The cheapest sound boards have a single chip or a pair of chips that recreate MIDI sound by synthesizing it. These can sound anywhere from really cheesy to pretty darn good, depending on the type and number of chips being used for the synthesis.

Better-quality sound boards mix MIDI technology with Wave. Instead of synthesizing the sound from scratch using simple mathematic algorithms, Wave Table sound cards actually store samples of real instruments in ROM on the board. Top-of-the-line sound boards can have up to two megabytes of sampled instrument sounds on the card, which are used for MIDI playback so good that you'll be looking for the orchestra pit.

Video Capture and Playback

The MPEG player board is next. Remember to install it next to the video controller, because you're going to need that interconnect cable to the "feature connector" on the video board. As we said before, you can buy MPEG players for less than $100 if you shop carefully. MPEG players are typically 16-bit ISA boards, so nothing special is required here.

Video e-mail or Videoconferencing? Make room for the video capture board. This is the board that connects to the external camera and/or microphone. Again, the image capture board is available as a 16-bit ISA board or for MicroChannel, and you can put them in just about any PC.

For certain manufacturers this board may replace the MPEG player board. If it does, remember to leave room next to the VGA adapter for the aforementioned feature connector.

There's one really big potential problem here. What if you want to support MPEG playback as well as H.320-based videoconferencing? Under current technologies you can't do this. Both the H.320 board and the MPEG board will expect access to your VGA card's feature adapter. Sorry, only one to a customer, so you'll have to decide which computers get which capabilities.

Network Adapters

As we've been going through the parts of the computer it may have become apparent to you that (except for real-time videoconferencing) you can use pretty much any multimedia technology with any style of computer that you have on the network, as long as it's a reasonably late-model machine. This is indeed true, but it's only part of the picture.

Remember that if you load up a computer with all the goodies, you're getting perilously close to the maximum throughput that machine can handle, especially when it comes to getting information onto and off of the network. That's fine but what if you have 10, 20, or 100 of these computers?

What you've done is saturate the network. Even though individual computers will work just fine, cumulatively nothing will work at all. There just isn't enough room on the network cable to carry the load for everyone, so some applications won't work properly, some won't work at all, and you run the very real risk of crashing the server because of overload.

That's why the network style and network adapters you choose are so important. If you're going to have networked multimedia, you will need *both* the multimedia *and* the network.

Logic will tell you that it's absolutely critical that you pay as much attention to the network as to the computers attached to it. If you work on the computers but not the network, you'll have incredibly sophisticated machines that can't actually do anything. If you work on the network but not the computers, you'll end up with the fastest word processors in the known universe but you won't have gotten to collaborative computing.

There are a tremendous number of network types, styles, and speeds, and picking the right one for your setup is so important that we're going to spend the remainder of this chapter talking about it.

NETWORK TOPOLOGIES AND SPEEDS

ARCnet

ARCnet is pretty much gone by now. It has gotten so old, in fact, that it is now a fairly expensive network type. One of the most important factors in how much something costs is how many of those somethings are being made and sold. If you make a lot of them you can sell a lot of them and the unit cost and price go down. If you're only making a few, the unit cost stays high and you have to charge more.

Since the only people making ARCnet purchases these days are usually making replacement purchases for components of LANs that have died, ARCnet pieces remain pretty expensive—usually almost twice as expensive as Ethernet and Token Ring, both of which are several times faster and more capable.

If your current network is ARCnet based, I'm really, truly sorry. Not a single one of the technologies discussed in this book will work for you. ARCnet is only capable of pushing 2.5 million bits per second of information across the LAN, and that's just not going to be fast enough for networked multimedia.

Actually, ARCnet is even slower than its raw speed would indicate. Because it is a "Token Passing Bus" interface, a large part of the network capacity is used up in system messages, known as *overhead*. On the average 40-station network, this means that each workstation has a real data carrying capacity of around 30,000 bytes per second, just barely faster than a floppy drive. Not good at all, and if you want to use any of the goodies we've been talking about, you're going to need to upgrade to Ethernet or Token Ring.

Ethernet

Ethernet is currently the most popular of the LAN technologies, and it's certainly the least expensive. This topology has been around for quite a while, too. Invented by Bob Metcalfe in the early 1970s, Ethernet has a raw data carrying rate of 10,000,000 bits per second. It's actually capable of double that, but "full-duplex" Ethernet never really caught on in the early days because the computers used were too slow to deal with that much information. In the past few years, a few companies have introduced full-duplex network adapters, but they're still pretty expensive.

One of the things that the industry likes about Ethernet is that it's fully standardized, allowing users to add equipment from any one manufacturer, secure in the knowledge that it will work with equipment from any other manufacturer. The original form of Ethernet was known as IEEE 802.3 Project 10Base5. In English this means that it's the International Electrical and Electronics Engineers (IEEE) Project Committee 802.3 for 10 millions bits per second over baseband at up to 500 meters or around 1,600 feet (10Base5). It quickly became known as simply "Thicknet."

Thicknet uses a bus shape with a big, thick RG-8 coaxial cable and requires a special device called a transceiver wherever you want to attach a device to the network. The network segment can be up to 500 meters long, and you can attach up to 100 devices to each segment. If you need more, you can attach multiple segments by tying them together through a repeater. Even though it's difficult and expensive to install, Thicknet is incredibly reliable, and one of the most common places to find it today is in the bowels of United States Navy ships.

"Thin" Ethernet

After a few years of dealing with Thicknet, market pressures forced the IEEE to come up with a simpler, cheaper way of creating an Ethernet network. The IEEE responded by creating 802.3 10Base2. 10Base2 uses thinner, cheaper RG-58 cable that is very similar to that used for cable TV installations. Because the cable is thinner, it has less bandwidth, so you are only allowed up to 32 devices per segment and the segment can only be 200 meters, or about 600 feet, in length. Multiple segments can still be attached through repeaters.

The biggest difference with 10Base2 is that it does not require a transceiver on the cable for each attached device. The transceiver circuit is much smaller and a great deal more simplified; and is provided on the network adapter itself. This convenience quickly earned it the term "Cheapernet."

10BaseT Ethernet

As popular as Thicknet and Cheapernet became, they have been almost completely supplanted by the current version of Ethernet: IEEE 802.3 10BaseT. "10BaseT" is the common name for this version, and it means 10 million bits per second on baseband over twisted-pair cable, or common business-grade phone cable.

Again, it was the market that drove the standard. Users realized that there was a tremendous amount of telephone cable already inside the walls of many companies, either completely unused or holding extra wire pairs. Most business telephone systems these days only use a single pair of wires, or at most two pairs, but most telephone cable installers use four-pair cables. This means that half the wires in the cable are up for grabs.

All of this conspired to change the shape of Ethernet as we know it. While 10Base5 and 10Base2 were bus topologies, with all the stations aligned along a single length of cable, 10BaseT is a star topology, with all the stations at the ends of their own individual cables, tied together through a hub. The hub is actually a multipoint repeater, and in essence what we're doing is putting each workstation and server on its own individual LAN segment.

When it was initially introduced, 10BaseT was quite expensive. The adapter cards for the desktops were about the same price as Cheapernet cards, but the hubs cost an arm and a leg or, more accurately, about $200 per individual workstation port. Nowadays you can buy an 8-port hub for less than $200, making the current price per port only $25. The price of adapter cards has fallen tremendously, too. The original Ethernet cards for PCs cost in the range of $300 each. If you are willing to buy them 20 at a time today, you can get them for $75 or less.

Full-Duplex Ethernet

There are several variations on the Ethernet theme. As we've already discussed, Ethernet can actually handle simultaneous transmission and reception, and full-duplex Ethernet networks that are capable of 20 million bits per second of throughput are available.

Only one little problem with the technology, though. Most networks that use Ethernet require that the receiving station send and acknowledgment whenever it receives a packet of data intact, and usually the sender waits until that acknowledgment is received before it sends the next packet, rendering full-duplex effectively useless.

Switched Ethernet

The other major variation on the theme is called "Switched Ethernet." Every single packet of data on the network carries a header that says who it's from and where it's bound. On a standard Ethernet network that packet is repeated to all segments and to all computers on that segment, and the stations that it's not intended for simply don't "listen" to the data. This uses up bandwidth fairly rapidly, especially on large networks.

If you want to increase throughput on your network, instead of a hub you use a switching hub. The switching hub is a computer in its own right that examines the headers of all the packets it receives and makes sure that those packets are only repeated on the segments that the recipient is actually on. You use a very fast cabling method to attach the server to the switching hub, like ATM, FDDI, or Fast Ethernet, and the hub grabs the packets, sorts them, and delivers them to the appropriate segments.

This results in speed gains that can be many times the original "unswitched" speed of the LAN. Each individual workstation is free to work at up to its full rated capacity without having to worry about sharing bandwidth on its segment with other devices. The only place where you have to think about capacity issues is on the high-speed connection between the hub and the server.

Isochronous Ethernet

This is the hybrid that we talked about earlier in this chapter. Isochronous Ethernet operates at 10 megabits per second for data and 6.144 megabits per second for voice and video simultaneously over the same type of network cable (twisted-pair telephone-type cable) as 10BaseT Ethernet.

To get the full 16 Mbps you must use special hubs and cards for the personal computers attached to the network. Computers with regular 10BaseT cards will work, but will not be able to take advantage of the added voice and video bandwidth.

Token Ring

Token Ring was introduced in the early 1980s by IBM. Its original operating speed was 4 million bits per second, and it was billed as a secure, reliable alternative to ARCnet that did not suffer from ARCnet's overhead problems. Realistically, Token Ring had enough problems of its own at that point.

First of all, it was expensive. Arranged in a "star wired ring," each workstation needed expensive, very difficult to install shielded twisted-pair cable from the workstation to the "Media Access Unit," or MAU. MAUs were expensive, and there were some very complicated calculations that limited the number of MAUs on the network, the distance between them, and the distance between MAUs and workstations. Add to that the fact that Token Ring was expensive when it was new, as adapters for workstations cost around $1,000 each. All of these conspired to keep Token Ring in the shadow of both ARCnet and Ethernet.

The first problem to be solved was cabling. It became possible to use Token Ring over standard unshielded twisted-pair (UTP—the same stuff that was later used for 10BaseT), but only if you were willing to cut the maximum distances on the network in half. It turned out that trying to use UTP over maximum distances introduced a noise problem called "jitter" onto the network that resulted in severe communications difficulties.

The second problem to be solved was speed. Since Ethernet was so much faster than Token Ring, the Token Ring designers set out to make it even faster than Ethernet. What they ended up doing was quadrupling the speed, to 16 millions bits per second. Now *this* was desirable, and Token Ring started to gain some momentum in the market.

Such a pity it didn't last too long. It turned out that the jitter problem was much worse at 16 megabits per second than it was at 4. For some large networks, the calculated maximum distance from MAU to workstation was less than 20 feet, which didn't do a whole lot of good. The problems were eventually solved by using better noise filters on the adapters and improving the network timing, but many of these changes came too late to help Token Ring take over from Ethernet.

Token Ring has other benefits, though, such as the fact the network performance doesn't degrade when you add additional workstations (aside from the natural slowdown that occurs when you attach a slew of computers to a single server). Both ARCnet and Ethernet will slow down when the network becomes large, regardless of server load. Token Ring also has built in protection against network disruptions and protects itself when a network adapter "goes insane." For this reason, Token Ring seems to be the network type of choice for banks and other financial institutions.

Next-Generation Technologies: The Need for Speed

As we have said all along, the most pressing issue to face when considering networked multimedia is bandwidth, or the total information carrying capacity of the cabling method. Ethernet and Token Ring can do some networked multimedia today, but as your users' interest in sound and video grows, you're going to be constrained. Perhaps its time to look at upgrading your network's speed now, before it becomes an issue.

Be careful, though, because it's not just the network cable and adapters. The network types you'll read about here are so fast that they often require the absolute latest technology in the PC (especially on the expansion bus, as we discussed earlier) in order to gain any advantage.

In this Corner, Fast Ethernet

Let's give a big networking "Hello" to Fast Ethernet and 100BaseVG-AnyLAN. Both of these topologies are vying to become "the next Ethernet." Fast Ethernet is just that—Ethernet on steroids, its official title is 100BaseT. Operating at 100 megabits per second, Fast Ethernet has all the best features of Ethernet, including the ability to work on the same twisted-pair cable as 10BaseT does (as long as the cable is the best grade available, called Category 5, if you need to run over 50 meters or 150 feet from the hub to the workstation), full-duplex capability, and switching hubs.

Most hubs currently on the market are called 10/100 hubs, in fact. This means that you can plug in either a standard 10-megabits-per-second Ethernet adapter or a 100-megabits-per-second Fast Ethernet card, and the hub can tell the difference and adjust its speed to match. This can allow you to mix old and new adapters on the same network.

In the Challenger's Corner, 100BaseVG-AnyLAN

Fast Ethernet's major competitor is 100BaseVG-AnyLAN. The major difference between the two is in the way they handle conflict between adapters trying to use the network simultaneously. Both Ethernet and Fast Ethernet use Carrier Sense Multiple Access with Collision Detection (CSMA/CD). When two adapters try to use a segment simultaneously, they both hear the other talking, shut up, and wait a random amount of time before trying to transmit again. This is called a collision. 100BaseVG uses Demand Priority Access Mode (DPAM) instead of CSMA/CD to make sure that all transmissions reach their intended destination and to reduce cable conflict.

FDDI/CDDI

The Fiber Distributed Data System (FDDI) is another 100-megabits-per-second network topology. As its name implies, it uses fiber optic cable carry the data around the network. FDDI is similar in organization to Token Ring, in that the actual cabling is a "star wired ring." FDDI has been around for a while, but because of the cost of adapters (over $1,000 each), hubs ($400 a port), and cabling (around $2 a foot), it hasn't really caught on.

If you want to talk about bad timing, then look no further than CDDI. The Copper Distributed Data System was an attempt to make FDDI less expensive by providing the same speed and capabilities over unshielded twisted-pair (telephone) cable. The only difference between FDDI and CDDI is the maximum distance between the workstation and the hub. Fiber optic is not sensitive to electrical or radio frequency interference, so you can typically run cables of 1 mile or more between workstation and hub. The proponents of CDDI argued that since most workstations are within 150 feet, or 50 meters, of the hub, cutting the maximum distance in return for using cheap cable and less expensive adapters and hubs was worth it. They were right, but their timing stank.

CDDI came to the market at about $600 per adapter card, with hub costs of about $250 per port, and running over cable that cost about $0.15 per foot. Unfortunately, CDDI showed up right at the same time that people started talking about Fast Ethernet, which would run at the same speed and cost about half of what CDDI cost. That was the end of the story for CDDI.

Asynchronous Transmission Mode (ATM)

What if 100 megabits per second isn't fast enough? The next step up is 155, using Asynchronous Transmission Mode, or ATM. ATM is a switched technology, where every packet of data is routed directly from the origination point to the recipient so that overall network capacity is less affected. It also endorses the concept that "smaller is better" in the way that the packets themselves are organized.

If you're using ARCnet, each packet of data on the network is fixed in size at 508 bytes, regardless of its contents. A simple keystroke response to a yes/no question is going to be over 500 bytes of empty space. Ethernet uses variable-size packets of 64 to 1,514 bytes, and Token Ring uses variable-size packets of up to 4,096 bytes. On the other hand, ATM uses fixed-size packets that are only 53 bytes long, making the time interval to switch an ATM packet through the network very short.

ATM has lots of growth built in to it. Currently you can buy ATM adapters and hubs that move data at 25 megabits per second (IBM's Nways equipment), 35 megabits per second, and 155 megabits per second. In the future, you will be able to go all the way up to 2.1 billion bits per second, which would, of course, be massive overkill for today's microcomputers.

The downside of using ATM is that the faster versions (155 megabits per second and above) require fiber optic cable all the way to the desktop. Not too many buildings come prewired with multimode fiber cable these days, so to implement ATM you're looking at a very expensive cabling job.

ON THE NETWORK SERVER

What do we have to do to the network server to support all this stuff? On the hardware side you'll have to set up the server to support whatever network topology you have chosen and make sure that it runs as quickly as possible. That's really about it, but if you put your server together intelligently, there are some opportunities to make life on the network, better, faster, and cheaper.

RAM

As with the workstation, you're going to need a lot of RAM. Most network operating systems take the disk directories of shared volumes and copy them into RAM to speed up searches and retrievals. The more hard-disk storage you have, the more RAM you're going to need.

Server-based applications, especially on Novell NetWare networks, take up a lot of RAM. Individual applications that require one, two or four megabytes of RAM for their own use are not uncommon.

Typical multimedia-enabled servers with appropriate levels of disk space and enough RAM to run multimedia server applications such as CTI have at least 32 megabytes of RAM, with 64 megabytes providing a comfortable margin of error.

If you're going to load this much memory into your server, you may have to upgrade its main board for two reasons: If it's an older server, it may not support more than 16 megabytes (lots of early 486 servers have this problem), and even if it does support more than 16 megabytes logically, it may not be physically able to do so.

Stuffing that much RAM into a server requires the use of 16-megabyte SIMM memory modules, and not all machine types support that module size. The general rule of thumb is that the later the model, the safer you are. Check with your server's manufacturer for the last word.

Hard Drives

A significant upgrade to the amount of disk storage space is probably in the cards for you, but that's not nearly as big a deal as it used to be. A major manufacturer has started shipping 9-gigabyte drives (that's 9 billion, or 9,000,000,000 bytes!) for less than $3,000 each.

Just five years ago that much storage would have come to you in 13 disk drives costing over $17,000. Many of us would have trouble finding the space for that many drives, let alone the money to buy them.

If you're going to add a lot of hard-drive capability to the server, there are two things you should take into account. First, consider seriously putting those drives outside the server's CPU case. Each drive you add to the system takes up a certain amount of room and generates a certain amount of heat. Add too many drives to the server, and you run the risk of either overloading the power supply or making it so hot inside the server that thermal drive failures occur.

For an extra $100 you can put that drive in its own case, with its own power supply. This is really cheap insurance when you think about the time and expense to replace a failed hard drive and restore all that data from tape backup. You do have tape backup, don't you?

The second consideration is not only to add storage to the network but to make that added storage more secure as well. Instead of adding one or two drives, consider adding five in a RAID array. The Redundant Array of Inexpensive Disks (RAID) specification allows you to use up to five cheap IDE hard drives per array, organized so that any one drive can fail and the system will keep operating with no loss of data whatsoever. You can remove and replace the failed drive while the disk assembly is still running (called Hot Swap), and when the new drive is installed the system will automatically reconstruct its data from information stored on the other four drives.

How does it do that? Each byte of information is actually written to all five drives. The first four get two bits each, and the fifth drive gets two parity bits. If any one drive fails, the system's logic can figure out what's missing from the remaining data and parity information. This is called RAID Level 5. There are lesser levels of redundancy and safety, with lower cost associated with each.

RAID is a really cheap technology for the level of safety that it buys you. If you use the new 2-gigabyte IDE hard drives, you can store up to eight gigabytes at a cost of around $6,000 per assembly ($1,000 per drive plus $1,000 for the RAID chassis and software). Figure 3.2 is an example of a RAID array, Micropolis Corporation's RAIDION.

Figure 3.2   Micropolis' RAIDION RAID array. Photo courtesy of Micropolis Corporation.

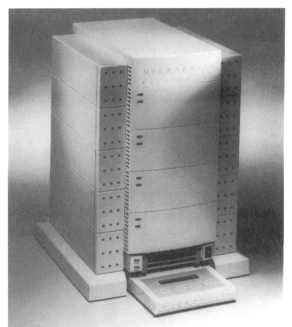

Shared CD-ROM

We've already talked about the impossibility of adding CD-ROM drives to every workstation and buying tons of copies of CD-ROM-based software. Starting a library of CD-ROMs is out, too, as almost no network manager has the time to administer such a program.

The answer is the CD-ROM server, which can be either software or hardware, or a combination of the two, and can take one of four forms. Just like file servers, these devices make CD-ROM-based programs and information available across the network. Costs range from nonexistent to outrageous.

If you have a NetWare 3.x or 4.x server, and you only need one or two CD-ROM drives with just a few users accessing them simultaneously, you can use Novell's own CD-ROM NetWare Loadable Module (NLM). This driver makes one or more CD-ROM drives available across the network as additional volumes. The NLM is provided with NetWare, so the only cost is for the drive and controller. This is the simplest and least expensive solution.

What if you have a bunch of CD-based software, but only a few people access each program at any given time? You are probably a candidate for nondedicated shared workstation access. That's a mouthful, but it represents a fairly simple idea. Let's say that on your 40-workstation network you have five PCs with CD-ROM drives. You can install software on each of these five machines that makes their CD-ROMs accessible across the network to other users. Bob Jones in Accounting might become the server for all the WordMulcher users, and Susan Johnson in Sales might become the server for all the users who need access to the mailing list database you purchased.

The software is small, efficient, and impacts the performance of the host computer only minimally. You can limit the number of simultaneous users to further control how the host computer is affected, and this method of access can also serve as a primitive form of license control, preventing more users than you have legitimate licenses for from using the software at the same time. An excellent example of this form of CD-ROM server is Opti-Net 4, from Reed Technology and Information Services, Inc.

The major benefit of using nondedicated shared workstation access is that you already have the server and it's already connected to the network. The new CD-ROM drives simply appear as additional volumes on the network and can quickly be "mapped" to drive letters on the client PCs, just like the A: floppy drive and the C: hard drive. Most network servers have capacity that is untapped, as it seems to be a common thing for network managers to buy more server than they really need.

The next step up is going to be a nondedicated CD-ROM server. This is typically achieved by adding multiple CD-ROM drives and sophisticated controller software to an existing network server. There are versions available for all the major network operating systems from a variety of vendors, including Reed's Opti-Net 4 NLM for NetWare, and Procom Technology's CD-Tower integrated drive and software packages (Figure 3.3).

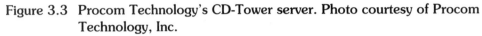

Figure 3.3   Procom Technology's CD-Tower server. Photo courtesy of Procom
             Technology, Inc.

More CD-ROMs? More users? You're going to need a dedicated CD-ROM
server. You can purchase complete systems, preconfigured, from companies
like Procom and Logicraft, or you can create your own CD-ROM server
hardware and use CD-View, from Ornetix Corp. CD-View actually creates a
server that appears as a NetWare version 2.2 "compatible" server on the
network. You administer it using all the NetWare tools you're already familiar
with, like SYSCON and FILER. Each CD-ROM drive is a volume on the server
and is accessed via Novell's MAP command, just like any other volume.

One unexpected benefit of using network-based CD-ROM is that you don't
need additional software at the workstation most of the time. Local CD-ROM
drives require Microsoft's CD-ROM Extensions (MSCDEX.EXE) and a

hardware driver. Network drives are addressed using good old NETX and MAP.

There's always going to be a "gotcha," and this is no exception. CD-ROM drives store programs, data, sound, and video—lots of video, which has to be delivered to the workstation at 300,000 bits per second or faster. This is going to eat bandwidth like candy, and if you have many users accessing CD-ROM across the network simultaneously, the network is going to run extremely slowly. Faster topologies like Fast Ethernet, 100BaseVG-AnyLan, FDDI, or ATM are a must.

Computer–Telephony Interfaces

There are several styles of CTI for the network server, but the most popular is already built in. Most computer telephony interfaces for network servers use the simple, neglected, and oft-maligned RS-232 serial port that your server probably already has several of.

A couple of systems using the TAPI interface require their own proprietary expansion board, but most of the time you won't need anything special in the server other than an open expansion port for the board and enough RAM to load the software.

Many network managers are afraid to hook up anything to their server's serial ports. There are several reasons for this. Early versions of network operating systems for personal computers didn't handle the serial port very well and were prone to crashes when things weren't exactly perfect on the port. This problem has been solved for some time, but attitudes persist.

The other reason for the network gurus' reluctance is that the serial port was sometimes used to attach modems for access from the outside world. This can be a security nightmare and did result in some very nasty occurrences way back in the dim and misty past.

Neither of these excuses are valid when it comes to using the server's serial port for computer–telephone integration, so you can smooth the network person's ruffled feathers with calm words of assurance.

WIDE AREA NETWORKS

Most wide area networks really aren't wide. By definition, a true WAN has the resources at one site and the consumers of those resources at other sites. What most of us have is a group of interconnected LANs, and this can be a problem when it comes to multimedia.

The reason is that same bugaboo that has popped up in so many places in this book already: bandwidth. Because we can't own the lines between remote sites, we have to lease capacity either from the local telephone company or from a long-distance company, and it's expensive—really, really expensive. So what do we do to minimize the expense? We cut down on the bandwidth, that's what.

Let's say you have a pair of Ethernet networks 200 miles apart, and both operate at 10 megabits per second. If you want to connect them at their "native" speed, you need to sign up for Synchronized Multimegabit Data Service, or SMDS. Guess how much that will cost. $500 per month? No way. $1,000 per month? Dream on. A 200-mile SMDS link will cost you around $7,000 per month. Very few companies can afford that kind of hit to the bottom line, so you look at reducing both the cost and the bandwidth.

Unfortunately, the next step down is 1.544 megabits per second, too slow for some networked multimedia applications, like multipoint videoconferencing. It's also pretty darned expensive, as it will cost you around $2,000 per month for that same 200-mile link. You can cut the speed in half, but the cost only drops by 40 percent—not terribly cost effective.

The next major step down is a very, very long one: 56,000 bits per second, too slow for any real-time multimedia applications. You can still use sound- and video-enabled e-mail, but actually looking at someone at the same time they're doing the talking is O-U-T. The costs do drop to a manageable level, though. That 200-mile link will run you about $400 per month.

The above is by way of illustration of some of the difficulties. We'll talk about the actual wide area networking technologies in the next chapter. For now, let's assume that you are either rich and have big bandwidth, or poor and have reconciled yourself to the fact that some multimedia technologies are going to be out of reach. In either event you still need to actually hook those networks up to each other.

Bridges and Routers: Traffic Cops on the Data Highway

All network types have limitations. Some limit the total number of devices that you can have attached. Others place limitations on the total distance from one end of the network to the other or between two devices on that network. Still others do both.

So what do you do if you run up against one of these limitations? You construct a second network and tie the two of them back together with a bridge or router. Since each network has its own workstations, servers, and applications, you can't just slap the two of them together with a ball of string and some chewing gum. You'll have to do it with technology, and that means bridges or routers.

If you had two networks that you wanted to bring together, you'd attach a single bridge to both of them. The bridge watches over multiple network segments, keeping track of the packets that flow across the cable. Each packet carries the network address of its recipient, and the bridge makes sure that packets are sent only to the segment where the addressee resides.

If a packet starts on one network and is to be delivered to an address on the same network, there's no reason to send it across the other network as well. No one there wants it, no one needs it, and they're all going to ignore it. It just takes up bandwidth that could be better used for something else. In a wide area environment, this prevents packets that are supposed to be staying local from being repeated across the WAN link and gumming up the legitimate traffic.

To use a metaphor, think of the packet as a letter and the bridge as a post office. The letter will travel from the sender through one or more post offices and then be given to the mail carrier who delivers for your street (the destination segment). On a computer network all of this is done automatically, as bridges actually watch network traffic and "learn" the addresses that are present as they go.

Bridges don't have to connect just two networks together. There are a number of brands that can accommodate 5, 10, or 100 separate networks all coming together from near and far. These meganetworks may have hundreds or even thousands of personal computers with billions of bits of data flowing across all the cables at any given time. They aren't always spread way out, either. In southern California the San Onofre Nuclear Power Generating plant has 12,000 workstations within a two-square-mile area. Now *that's* a network.

Bridges come in two types: local and remote. Local bridges have two or more "ports" of the same type (usually Ethernet or Token Ring) and are there simply to cut down the amount of extraneous traffic on really big LANs. Remote bridges are used to connect a LAN to a WAN and typically have two ports. One port is whatever your local area network is, and the other is a high-speed serial port. The most common type is V.35, which can be used for anything from 9,600 up to 1,544,000 bits per second. Other types are RS-530, RS-442, and RS-449. Conspicuously absent is RS-232, the standard PC serial port type, which is only reliable at up to 128,000 bits per second.

Routers are essentially really smart bridges that are typically used for large WANs. In addition to looking at network traffic and deciding which packets to pass on, they communicate with other routers on the network. In doing this they figure out the most efficient way to deliver packets that are supposed to be out on the WAN. The routers all cooperate to send data packets down the shortest possible route from origin to destination.

This routing capability helps make your network more robust as well. If one router fails, the rest of them take note of that failure and cooperate in rerouting network traffic around the breach. When the dead router is resurrected the network is "healed" and normal traffic resumes.

For wide area networking this makes routers quite a bit more desirable than "mere" bridges. For example, a bridge only knows if a packet is supposed to

Figure 3.4 The Ascend Pipeline 50 wide area router.

be "in" or "out." A router knows not only that but also which other remote routers are supposed to get that packet, allowing you to construct a network that looks a lot more like a matrix than a pipeline. Figure 3.4 shows Ascend's Pipeline 50 wide area router.

All of these devices are necessary to get multiple LANs talking to each other. In the next chapter we'll deal with the wide area links themselves.

4
SERVICES FOR THE WIDE AREA NETWORK

In order to have a wide area network, you have to have some method of getting data from point A to point B. This chapter discusses the various methods along with their relative costs and benefits.

Dial-Up Multimedia

I f you already have a computer, you have the minimum basic requirement
for wide area networking: a telephone. Ever since the dawn of the computer
age people have been using phone lines to hook multiple computers together.
All it takes is the line, a computer with a serial communications port, and a
device called a modem. Using a regular phone line and modem is called
"dial-up" because that's exactly what you do. You (or your computer) use
the phone to dial up another computer in order to communicate.

Modem is the contraction of *Modulator/Demodulator*. A modem is a box (or
a card that fits into the computer) that turns data bits into audible yodels and
shoves them across the phone line to the other end, where another modem is
waiting to turn the yodels back into bits again. The earliest modems were
acoustic types that actually clipped on to the handset of your telephone,
yodeled into the microphone, and listened to the speaker like a kind of
demented cyber-dwarf. That's not the way we do it anymore, though. Virtually
all modems manufactured in the last ten years jack straight into the phone line.

You can get a surprising amount of data across that phone line. The latest
generation of modems move data at 28,800 bits per second. If the modems at
either end are really, truly compatible with each other, they will negotiate data
compression at the beginning of the conversation, and the data rate can jump
as high as 115,200 bits per second. The modem at one end looks at the data
as it enters via the serial port and uses a mathematical formula to squish it
down by eliminating most repetitions and redundancies. The squished data is
transmitted across the phone line, and the modem at the other end unsquishes
it by applying the same formula in reverse.

Since 115,200 bits per second is quite fast in the world of wide area
networking, you would think that this would be a pretty good way to do
multimedia, wouldn't you? Unfortunately, it isn't. The reason is that most
really large data streams like JPEG photographs and MPEG video are already
compressed. When you try to move them across a compressed modem link,
the modem's compression looks at the data and throws its hands up in disgust.

"I can't compress something that's already compressed!" it cries, and the image or movie crosses the wire at the rather pokey 28,800-bits-per-second rate.

So, what kind of multimedia can you do across a modem line? Whiteboard applications work great, so weekend teleconferences from home are a definite possibility. For anything else you can forget about real time and you better not be in a hurry. Sound and video e-mail are still possibilities, but remember that the 2-megabyte, 3-minute video recording you left for the CEO will take 10 minutes just to download to her computer.

Remember also, that as far as the phone company is concerned, this is just another phone call, for which it will be happy to take your money. If it's a long-distance phone call, those ten minutes are going to cost you an appreciable amount, so it would be wise to think carefully about just which multimedia services you're going to allow across dial-up lines.

The dial-up network itself also imposes certain limitations. When you make a phone call, it is switched from one end to the other. Depending on how far away the recipient of the call is, the data can be making its way through anywhere from 1 to 50 telephone company switching stations. Each time the signal passes through one of these stations it gets slowed down a tiny amount and a small amount of noise is added to the signal. Eventually you get to a point where there's either too much delay or too much noise and the circuit is no longer usable for data communications.

Satellite phone calls are death on data communications. Since the satellite is hanging there in space (the real kind, not cyberspace) 22,300 miles up, even traveling at the speed of light your data is going to take a quarter of a second to make the trip up, over, and down. If you send a data packet and are waiting for a reply, it's not going to arrive for at least a half a second. Multiply that half-second by the thousands or tens of thousands of packets in an average data communications session, and you'll see that the only people who will be happy about this are at the phone company, which gets paid for all the seconds, not just the productive ones.

DEDICATED RESOURCES—LEASED LINES

O bviously, we need something better than dial-up lines. In order to get that something better, we have to shift away from analog lines using sound (remember the yodeling) to move data, toward digital communications that move the data in its native format. The simplest way to do this is to lease a digital circuit from the phone company. Since digital normally takes some preparation on the part of the telco, the most common digital circuits are point-to-point leased lines.

56K ADN Circuits

If there is a "most common" type of wide area link, this is it. 56K ADN is telephone company terminology for 56,000 bits per second on Advanced Digital Network. Because the industry is so fragmented today, you'll also hear it referred to in some parts of the country as 56K DDS, for Digital Data Service. It's the exact same thing, though.

A 56K circuit will cost you about $1,000 to install, and then you're going to have to pay either one or three companies a monthly fee for its use. If the link is "local" or within a single city, you'll pay the local telephone company between $100 and $400 a month.

If the link goes to another city, all of a sudden you have to look at it as having three separate parts. The section that goes from your office to the nearest long-distance carrier's Point of Presence (POP) is called the "local loop," and your local telephone company will receive between $100 and $300 a month, depending on the actual distance to the POP. The part of the line that runs from the local POP to the remote POP is called the InterExchange Carrier (IXC) portion, and you'll pay about 75 cents per mile per month for that. There's another local loop at the remote end waiting for your checkbook, too. Depending on how you ordered the circuit, you'll have to cut one or three checks each month.

A 56K circuit is popular for a number of reasons. The simplest and most important is that it's the cheapest way to tie multiple LANs together full-time at a reasonable speed. Another reason is that the equipment necessary to support 56K is simple, readily available, and inexpensive. All you need is a Customer Service Unit/Data Service Unit (CSU/DSU), which is essentially a translator between your kind of digital data and the telephone company's kind, a bridge or router, and a network connection. Put one of these setups on either end of the line, plug it in, and you are now a wide area networking expert.

The router may not even be necessary. Novell's NetWare supports the use of serial ports as network ports and you can connect the CSU/DSU directly to a late-model RS-232 port to use the server itself as the router. Be cautious about this approach, however, as it steals quite a few clock cycles from the server and may adversely affect performance on the local part of the network. An external router or a expansion board for your server that is a "router on a card" may be the better way to go, especially since many routers also perform on-the-fly compression that can boost your effective throughput to 192K, 256K, or even 384K bits per second.

With regard to networked multimedia, 56K is good enough for whiteboards and delayed transmission sound and video via e-mail. It is nowhere near good enough for videoconferencing, even simple point-to-point stuff. If you're using compression and think that you actually have three or four times that rate, think again. Videoconferencing data is already compressed, so the router won't be able to do much if anything to smoosh the data down further. It just won't work.

T1 and Fractional T1

If you're going to try to support real-time video, you're going to have to step up the pace. The next type of dedicated digital service is called T1 and it runs at 1,544,000 bits per second or slower.

T1 is actually divided up into 24 "virtual" channels by time slicing, and you can order just the portion that you need in 64,000-bits-per-second increments. You get the channels you pay for, and the telephone company is free to sell the unused portion to someone else. If you use less than the complete T1 circuit, it's called Fractional T1.

The IXC portion of a T1 circuit is very reasonably priced. In fact, it's not terribly more than a dedicated 56K line (which in all probability is really a single channel on the long-distance company's T1). It's the local loops that are going to hurt you. Because a local loop goes from the telephone company directly to you, nobody else gets to share the unused portion, and you have to pay for the whole thing regardless of whether you're using it or not.

To support T1 on your network you'll need a T1 CSU/DSU (Figure 4.1) that costs about $1,500 and a bridge or router with a high-speed serial port (almost certainly V.35). If you're going to use the whole T1 circuit the CSU/DSU can be a very simple one. If you're going to use Fractional T1, the device has to be more complex and the price jumps up. Fractional T1 CSU/DSUs can be configured in the field to use from 1 to all 24 virtual channels, so if you decide to increase your WAN bandwidth at a later date, your investment is protected.

Figure 4.1 The Adtran T1 CSU/DSU.

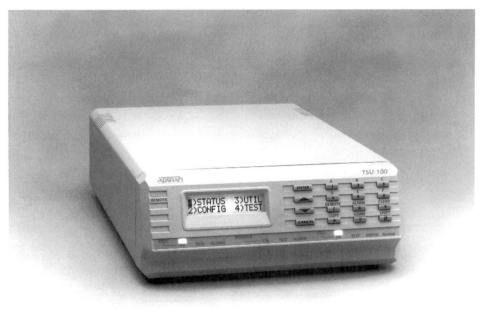

At what point does Fractional T1 become useful for multimedia? You can do whiteboarding and sound/video e-mail on a single channel, but that's very wasteful. You might as well have ordered a 56K line instead. For real-time applications you can get slow, jumpy video at 128K but have nothing left over for other network applications. You can get reasonably smooth video at 256K, but again there won't be anything left for the rest of the network.

At 384K you can have full-motion video for a single point-to-point videoconference and nothing else. In order to allow for additional "regular" net traffic, the slowest reasonable speed for Fractional T1 is 512K bits per second, or 8 virtual channels in the T1 pipeline. If you are going to support multipoint conferencing, you'll need to step up to full T1 and purchase all 24 channels.

Synchronized Multi-Megabit Digital Service (SMDS)

Are you extremely rich? Are you a large government agency or other "deep pockets"-type organization? If so, you may wish to consider a technology that turns your wide area network back into a local area network. Synchronized Multi-Megabit Digital Service (SMDS) is available at 4 megabits per second to match older Token Ring networks, 10 megabits per second to match Ethernet networks, and 16 megabits per second to match the current Token Ring generation. It's also available at slower speeds for organizations that want to mix fast and slow on a single network and at higher speeds (up to 45 megabits per second!) for organizations that want to tie multiple mainframe computers together.

SMDS is a fairly new technology based on the same technical specifications as those of Asynchronous Transmission Mode (ATM). At some point in the not too distant future, SMDS will become an external form of ATM and your network won't have boundaries anymore. Traffic will simply go wherever it's supposed to go, regardless of whether that's across the building, the city, or the country. Remember that ATM is a switched technology, so this is going to be one fast network.

SMDS is part of ATM, and ATM is part of SONET, the Synchronous Optical Network. The SONET specification allows for speeds of up to 2.1 billion bits per second of throughput, and there's actually a SONET network in use right now. It's used to connect the supercomputers at each of the six National Supercomputer Centers scattered around the country.

You're not going to need gigabit speeds, but you might be interested in the bottom of this line, SMDS. What does SMDS cost? How does a lock of your hair, three drops of blood, and your immortal soul sound? I'm joking. Relax!

SMDS *is* the most costly of the wide area technologies. A simple cross-town link at 10 megabits per second is going to cost approximately $4,500 a month. If that link needs to run to another city, you could be looking at double or triple that amount.

What can you do with multimedia over SMDS? Anything you want, including limited multipoint videoconferencing. Remember that the limiting factor here is likely to be the capabilities of the workstations, not the network itself.

PUBLIC DATA NETWORKS

Frame Relay

What used to be considered leading edge (some might say bleeding edge) is now a mature technology. Frame Relay can be a very cost-effective alternative to dedicated links, either 56K or T1/Fractional T1. With dedicated link technology you're renting a specific set of wires from your point of entry to your point of exit. Frame Relay reverses that concept, and what you are doing is leasing capacity on the vendor's network. How your data packets get from one end to the other is their responsibility.

You will be leasing a port on the Frame Relay network, which can be anywhere from 56,000 to 1,544,000 bits per second of capacity. The port gets a unique identifier, which is used to route data packets across the Frame Relay network. You can even set up a pseudo-dedicated link by using DLCIs, or Direct Link Connection Identifiers.

One nice thing about Frame Relay is that you can really size the network to your exact requirements. For example, let's say that you have four remote sites with 56K ports each. At your local site you don't need four ports to match the remote ports. Instead, you have one really big port, and you get to decide just how big it should be. If you think that the remote sites will be tossing data at full strength simultaneously, you set up a 256K port. If it is not likely that all the remote sites will be operating simultaneously, you reduce the local port size to 192K, 128K, or even 56K bits per second. If the remote sites do start pitching lots of data at home base, the "overrun" will be discarded by the network and the remote sites will have to retransmit the data later. This all happens automatically in the background, so you don't have to worry about manual intervention at any time.

If you're going to use Frame Relay, you need to be comfortable with two other terms as well. CIR, Committed Information Rate, is the rate at which the network provider promises to deliver your data. EIR, Excess Information Rate, is the rate at which the network provider says that it will make "best effort" to deliver your data. If the network fills up, you will receive the CIR's worth of data and the EIR packets will get pitched.

For all this you will pay for the ports, including the same local loop charges that you pay for dedicated links and sometimes for utilization. The higher the CIR, the more the port costs. Most of the long-distance carriers that offer Frame Relay charge for each packet (around one one-hundredth of a cent each), but put a cap on the maximum monthly charge for data. Sprint's cap is currently at $74 per month, for example. The regional Bells also offer Frame Relay service within their service areas, and Pacific Bell is currently flat-rating its service. Flat rating means that you pay for the port and the private virtual circuit only, with no packet data charges.

To install Frame Relay at your site you'll need much the same equipment that you would for dedicated links: A CSU/DSU for the local loop and a bridge or router. Since the links have identifiers that the network must see, the bridge/router must be Frame Relay compatible and you'll have a few extra setup steps at installation time.

On the networked multimedia side of the equation Frame Relay introduces some fairly thorny problems. The first problem has to do with the fact that Frame Relay is a packet-switched network. Your data is going to travel through two or more high-speed switches on the provider's network, and each switch will introduce some delay in the time it takes the packet to travel from one side of the network to the other. This travel delay is called latency, and it can cause problems with real-time applications.

The other major problem has to do with the CIR/EIR situation. Let's say that you have two Frame Relay ports, with a CIR of 512,000 bits per second and an EIR of 1,544,000 bits per second. You have a point-to-point videoconference in progress when all of a sudden someone starts a massive database query across the WAN. Your videoconference is being sequenced with the database query, so some of your packets are CIR and some are EIR. The Frame Relay network isn't busy, so you and the person at the other end don't even notice.

But suddenly the Frame Relay network gets busy, and your carrier cuts you back to the CIR and begins to drop EIR packets. The videoconferencing application is going to go crazy or stop working entirely. Frames will arrive incompletely or not at all, and the sound will get all beat up, too. Then it clears as the network quiets down and just as suddenly goes crazy again. If this is a regular occurrence on your network, you'll soon see villagers with torches and long sharp sticks making their way towards the MIS castle, coming to kill the monster you've created.

There are two possible solutions to this problem. The first is to increase the CIR until you have enough bandwidth so that no packets will ever be dropped. However, increasing the CIR increases its cost, so this option isn't ideal.

The other alternative is to reduce the EIR rate or even make the CIR and EIR the same number. If you do this, you're placing an artificial bottleneck on your wide area network, but at least performance will be uniform.

In summary, Frame Relay has definite benefits, especially in the area of cost containment, but use those benefits carefully. A poor setup can render the network useless for everyday activities.

Integrated Services Digital Network (ISDN)

In order to telecommute efficiently in the age of local area networks, the home worker has to be able to tie in to the office network and work as if he were right there with everyone else. Using established technology is prohibitively expensive because you have to create a 1-computer LAN at each telecommuting worker's home and then provide communications access to those tiny little LANs, usually with expensive leased lines from the telephone company.

You don't have to do that anymore. A new type of telephone line, called Integrated Services Digital Network (ISDN), allows remote locations to attach to LANs easily, quickly, and, above all, cheaply, at speeds that make it possible to do useful work and even support some forms of networked multimedia. There's a lot more information on ISDN and its uses in Chapter 4.

ISDN comes in two flavors: Basic Rate Interface (BRI) and Primary Rate Interface (PRI). The Integrated Services Digital Network is a second telephone network that lives right next door to the analog network that you and I use every time we make a phone call. The regular network is sometimes referred to as POTS (Plain Old Telephone Service. Who ever said that Ma Bell doesn't have a sense of humor?).

ISDN is a dial-up network just like POTS, but you're dialing digitally across a completely digital network. This means that calls are connected fast, usually in a half-second or less. ISDN BRI operates at 128K bits per second, divided up into three channels. There are two 56K-bit-per-second channels, called the B channels, and an 8K-bit-per-second channel for control signals, called the D channel, that is rarely if ever used. That's why BRI is also called 2B+D. Depending on how you dial the call, the two B channels can be multiplexed together to form a single 112K-bit-per-second channel using a built-in protocol called BONDING.

Primary Rate ISDN provides 1,544,000 bits per second of throughput, divided up into 24 B channels and 1 high-capacity D channel, so it's also called 24B+D. When you dial a long-distance PRI call, you specify how many channels to use, up to the total capacity of the line. You're charged standard business rates, including long-distance charges, on a per-channel basis, so a 24-channel call is like making 24 simultaneous phone calls.

Local ISDN calls are charged in one of two ways, depending on where you live in the country. Some RBOCs charge business rates for all calls made; others charge a flat rate per month regardless of the number of calls or their duration; and several allow for dedicated ISDN services. If your RBOC allows for this, it's a wonderful opportunity!

When dedicated ISDN BRI is available its a lot cheaper than 56K dedicated, even for 112K-bit-per-second 2-channel calls. You get twice the throughput at about 75 percent of the cost. Is there a downside? Only the fact that the equipment necessary to hook up to ISDN, which includes an ISDN modem and a network termination device called an NT1, is slightly more expensive than a CSU/DSU for 56K, but you'll still get that difference back in lower operating costs. The back end of the ISDN modem uses a high-speed serial port, and you'll need an ISDN router to attach it to your network (Figure 4.2).

Figure 4.2 The Advanced Computer Communications (ACC) Yukon ISDN router. Photo courtesy of Advanced Computer Communications, Inc.

ISDN PRI works in exactly the same way, but offers 12 times the throughput for around 5 times the cost. If flat-rated or dedicated service is available in your area, plain and simple, it's a deal. If all you can get is business rates, it might still be a deal, but you'll have to do a careful cost analysis, taking into account just how often the link will need to be up and how many channels you'll need to use.

Since ISDN is point to point, there are none of the latency or data discarding issues that make Frame Relay iffy in multimedia environments. Assuming that you have both the appropriate bandwidth and local PCs, you can use any multimedia technology with confidence.

THE INTERNET AS DELIVERY VEHICLE

I f this topic were any broader, we would have to put a "Caution: Wide Load" sign on the cover of this book. The Internet is a worldwide network of interconnected mainframes, minicomputers, and individual PCs all operating on a peer-to-peer basis and sharing information over the TCP/IP communications protocol.

The Internet does not operate at a single transmission speed. Instead, there are multiple "backbones" that move data at rates from 45 million to 2.1 billion bits per second. These backbones connect to National Access Points, or NAPS, and tie into thousands of slower connection links, which then tie into tens of thousands of even slower connection links, which then tie into... well, you get the idea. The overall effect is like the circulatory system of your body, with major veins, minor veins, and untold numbers of capillaries.

There are two kinds of backbone on the United States portion of the Internet. The biggest one is currently called the NSFnet and is supposed to be used for educational and governmental traffic only. A smaller one is called the Commercial Internet Exchange (CIX) and is available for any kind of traffic, as long as the Internet provider hooking into it pays its $10,000 per month. If you establish an Internet link, you don't have to pay the ten grand because the access provider that you're hooking into pays one fee for *all* of their customers.

How do you hook into the Net? There are dozens of ways, using all of the wide area technologies we've discussed to this point. The simplest is to dial into an Internet provider using a standard modem at 14,400 bits per second, or 28,800 bits per second if you have a new modem and your Internet provider supports this speed.

Links of 56K are available over dedicated circuits, Frame Relay, and ISDN BRI. Faster links are also available over dedicated circuits, Frame Relay, ISDN BRI, and SMDS. You'll need the same equipment that you use in attaching to a private network to attach to a Net provider.

A few companies have based their wide area networks on the Internet instead of establishing private networks, but there are some definite problems with this. One major problem is that the Internet uses a communications model that assumes that no transaction will reach its destination, and it's a happy surprise when it does. Of course, most transactions do reach their destinations or else the whole thing would break down, but it's a crummy model to run a business on.

Another problem is that the Internet experiences wide variations in performance because of its sheer size. Moving a packet of data from here to there can take milliseconds right now and minutes just a little while later. This is the death knell for most real-time applications.

The last and arguably most important problem is the nature of the Internet itself. It's not secure. In fact it's not even close to being secure and can be viewed as the "Wild, Wild West" of the information frontier. With thousands upon thousands of bored college students, HNGs (Horny Net Geeks), and other counterculture types as permanent residents, the Net records literally thousands of data intrusion attempts every single day.

Now that being said, the Internet offers a wealth of opportunity in multimedia. The major application used on the Net, the World Wide Web, is itself a multimedia application with text, images, and sound and motion video all used interchangeably and available across all types of computer systems.

Web applications are called documents even though they are really much more than that. A Web document is created using the *lingua franca* of the Net, the HyperText Markup Language, or HTML. Web browsers are used to connect to information providers and read, interpret, and display HTML documents. There are Web browsers available for every major and minor computer type, including PCs, Macs, UNIX workstations, and even mainframe terminals (which are limited to the text portion only). If the browser can't deal with an HTML feature like a video clip, it simply ignores it.

Applications are available on the Net for real-time voice conversations. One product for PCs with Microsoft Windows, called InterPhone, is taking off like wildfire. It allows you to conduct a point-to-point voice conversation across the Internet with any other InterPhone user, and all it requires is an Internet connection and a Windows PC with a sound board and microphone.

Quality is very good. If you have a standard Windows-enabled sound board, conversations are half-duplex, meaning that you talk, then they talk, then you talk, and so forth. If you have one of the new generation of sound boards that can record and play back simultaneously, then you can use Internet Phone in full-duplex mode just like a regular telephone. Examples of full-duplex sound boards include the Gravis UltraSound Max from Advanced Gravis Computer Technology; the ASB 16 Audio System from AdLib Multimedia, Inc.; and the Spectrum OfficeF/X from Spectrum Signal Processing, Inc. Complete vendor references for these and other companies are in the *Vendor Guide* in Appendix A.

The cost of the software is $99, and the calls are free. Yes, that's free—as in nothing, nada, zip, zilch—regardless of the length or distance of the call.

There is also a new application on the Net for real-time videoconferencing. It's called CU-SeeMe and was developed at Cornell University. The software is public domain (yes, there's that word *free* again), and it works across the PC, Macintosh, and UNIX X Windows platforms. Pretty well, too. All that is needed is a computer with a camera and image capture board and an Internet link of 56K or better. Images are black and white and appear in very small windows, but it gets the job done. There's additional information on this product in Chapter 8.

Would you want to use the Net for your business-critical multimedia needs? Probably not, at least not yet. The wide variability of data transmission speeds, security issues, and the disposable nature of Net traffic make it less than desirable for the important stuff. You're better off evaluating the Net as a source of information that will help you and your users do their jobs more productively. The World Wide Web is an incredible source of information on every topic from academia to business to finance to government, with over 100,000 Web servers in operation and new ones arriving at the rate of 3,000 per week. Global electronic mail to over 20 million Net users is an attraction, and new Net multimedia tools are cute, fun to play with, and may have business applications in the near future. Better keep an eye on things, as this is likely to be the hot topic of the 90s.

COMMERCIAL VIDEOCONFERENCING FACILITIES

If you want the benefits of videoconferencing but you're not ready to pay the freight to add it to your network, you do have one other option: using someone else's. At least one major long-distance carrier and one reprographics firm have commercial videoconferencing facilities available for rent by the hour. More companies are adding this capability on a daily basis, so check with your long-distance carrier for vendor references. The telephone companies all love this stuff because it's "value added," which means that the services aren't listed under their tariffs and they can charge as much as they want for them.

Sprint (the long-distance company) and Kinko's (the copy places) have fully appointed videoconferencing facilities available for rental. Prices start at $150 per hour per location and escalate from there, depending on the number of locations in the conference, how many cameras will be used at each site, and so on.

If the thought of at least $300 per hour ($150 times a minimum of two locations) doesn't scare you, then you might want to give this some serious consideration. A "test" conference offers the ability to try out this technology before you commit the time and dollar resources to implement it in house, and it exposes your users to the technology at the same time. Their responses and how well they use the system will tell you a lot about how likely they are to accept and embrace videoconferencing.

If you do decide to try a videoconference using rented facilities, make sure that you do it right. Plan for the meeting by preparing a more detailed agenda than you normally would. Make sure that the participants know the ground rules, including a strong admonition not to waste time on nonproductive issues. At $300 an hour, those can be some pretty expensive jokes.

Make sure that each site in the conference has a moderator, and that the moderator is prepared to keep things moving and on track. Have him or her give a brief talk before the camera lights go on about the purpose and nature of the meeting, and to remind participants of the rules.

For your own purposes try to debrief the participants either in person or by questionnaire within a couple of days after the meeting. Try to obtain both objective and subjective results while you're at it. Questions like "Did you accomplish your objective for the meeting?" and "Did you enjoy using this technology to accomplish your objectives?" are entirely appropriate.

If you set it up well and follow through, a test session can provide a wealth of information about the likely success or failure of an in-house effort.

5 REASONS AND RATIONALIZATIONS

Networked multimedia can be desirable in and of itself as far as individual people in the organization are concerned. Like moths to the flame, we are drawn toward new and exciting technologies. However, in the business world costs must be offset by benefits. This chapter discusses the benefits likely to accrue both within and outside the enterprise.

THE WHAT AND THE WHY

So far we've talked about all of these systems as if they were a kind of noncaloric candy that we can eat forever without getting fat or suffering an upset stomach. That's a nice thought, but unfortunately it's not corporate reality. In the real world we have to balance the benefits and possible productivity increases against the cost and possible productivity decreases.

Let's face it, a lot of this stuff is candy. Plenty of flash and glitter but of limited usefulness in the marketplace. The direct benefit of implementing a technology should be immediate, measurable, and noticeable. There may very well be indirect benefits, but about all we can do is take notice of them and list them for the edification and enjoyment of the people who actually read memos.

Now that we understand collaborative computing technologies themselves, we need to apply those technologies to the types of people we're likely to encounter in the workplace. We'll take a look at each of the different "classes" of worker in terms of how they approach their jobs and how they would be affected by the introduction of networked multimedia. Rather than discuss the ins and outs of a particular application or piece of hardware, we'll talk about how a class of worker is likely to use it (or not to use it) and what benefits are likely to accrue from its use.

It's probable that you're going to have to "sell" the need for these things to top management. Since the second most common question in any given person's mind is usually "What's in it for me?" (the most common question is "Where should I go for lunch?"), we'll start at the top and work our way down the corporate ladder.

EXECUTIVES AND MANAGERS

It seems that the higher you are in a company the more precious your time gets. Endless successions of meetings, conferences, and telephone calls all conspire to make time pass with disturbing quickness. And if the meetings and conferences require travel, that only makes it worse. Trips to the airport and time spent in transit are marginally unprofitable and very expensive, as cellular phones are often the only way to keep in touch. Even when you're in the office, having to make a trip to another manager's office interrupts your work flow and steals precious minutes.

If we can reduce or eliminate travel, then we can realize significant productivity gains. In this class it's the real-time multimedia components that will provide the most bang for the buck. Having access to a whiteboarding application will allow managers to compare notes (literally) when preparing for staff meetings or presentations. A quick phone call, a few keystrokes, and everyone's in sync with each other, preventing embarrassing missteps in front of customers or staff.

Executives are prime beneficiaries of groupware, although not as contributors. Because groupware provides centralized storage of important documents and projects, executives with proper access rights can keep their finger on the pulse of the business more readily by actually watching progress being made (or not made) on their pet projects. Couple this benefit to the tightly integrated e-mail aspect, and you can see that groupware has definite benefits here.

The same applies to multimedia presentation graphics. Execs are likely recipients of the technology's benefits rather than users of the technology itself. Not too many company presidents will sit down at the computer keyboard to create a multimedia presentation with animation and sound for the weekly staff meeting. Their secretaries might, but they won't.

On the other side of the coin most executives love *seeing* high-tech presentations. Partly it's the fact that multimedia is engrossing and they can always use the diversion. Partly it's the fact that they're jealous. In either event, using multimedia to present to the brass (If you use oom-pah music, are you presenting brass to the brass? Just wondering.) can make the presentation more favorably received.

Here's a paradox for you: Desktop videoconferencing is the most desirable multimedia tool for executives, but it's actually of the most limited utility. Desktop video is the sexiest of all the networked multimedia applications. It uses the highest levels of technology, costs an appalling amount and is a great way to say "I'm powerful" without saying a word. But who are you likely to be using it to talk to? Other executives who are probably just a few steps down the hall. This is not a good way to spend scarce capital funds.

On the other hand, putting video on the executive's desk is a terrific idea, but for video-enabled e-mail, not real time. Why? Because the most common complaint that top-level managers have is that they don't get enough "face time" with their lower-level employees. A few video e-mails sent to broad distribution lists to talk about specific issues or the overall state of the company are a very powerful tool for keeping morale high and employees "in the loop."

Remember that it doesn't take much to set up a desktop computer to *receive* video e-mail. A reasonably powerful computer with a sound board and the requisite software is all you need. Therefore, outfitting a select few with the ability to send video and a whole bunch with the ability to receive it can pay solid dividends.

So where does videoconferencing make sense? Anywhere you have the organization split geographically, and usually organized along departmental lines rather than by picking and choosing individual desktops. If your company is large enough to have different divisions at multiple locations, you're typically going to have meetings at the corporate office to keep everyone updated on what everyone else is doing. These meetings involve bringing people some distance, and they cost a lot, especially when you factor in the time of the people involved. Think how much easier it could be with a videoconferencing-equipped PC at each location in a commonly accessible spot like the conference room or the general manager's office. At the predetermined time everyone gathers in their respective conferencing locations, and the meeting proceeds as scheduled, but without any of the delays associated with airplanes and the costs associated with cellular phones.

Having a second computer in the room with a whiteboarding application will really speed things up and add another level of both productivity and pizzaz. Everyone can view notes, financial data, or presentations without squirming or straining, and the paper flow between offices is cut down significantly. See something on screen you need? Just select "print" and a few seconds later it quietly falls into the hopper of the laser printer down the hall.

Want to take it to yet another level? Hook the computer with the whiteboarding application to an LCD projection panel sitting on an overhead projector. Now everyone in the room can relax and watch the big screen without having to cluster around a dinky little monitor. A simple LCD projection system can be purchased for as little as $3,000 and it's portable. When you're not using it for meetings, you can lend it to Sales and Marketing personnel to take with them for presentations at customer sites.

SALESPERSONS

S peaking of the ever-popular sales force, where do they fit into the mix? Assuming that you use an outbound sales force (as opposed to an inbound sales force that's been shackled to the telephones), this group can be problematic because of their mobility. Good salespeople are rarely in the office, and the less time they spend at home base, the more productive they are likely to be.

How progressive is your company? Most organizations these days are pretty restrictive about giving computers to salespeople, and there are a couple of good reasons for that. It can be argued that the more time a salesperson spends fiddling with a computer, the less time he has available to meet with customers and actually sell things.

It can also be argued that most salespeople are not very computer literate and it takes too much effort and precious time to educate them to the benefits of computers. Both of these arguments are fairly valid, as the "state of the art" in terms of sales management software is still less than totally intuitive.

Let's argue this the other way. Assume that your sales force is intelligent, progressive, and forward thinking. Therefore, you have the ultimate in sales contact management software and each and every one of your field sales personnel has a shiny new subnotebook that is stuffed full of RAM, has a big old hard disk, and is equipped with the latest microprocessor. Now what?

The best connectivity to the network that you can offer them is ISDN access at 128 kilobits per second, and even that's not going to be widely available. The problem is that ISDN phone lines are about as common as UFO sightings and aren't likely to become more common until the millennium. The salespeople will have to fall back on 28,800-bit-per-second modems, and that's just too darn slow for most types of multimedia.

The exception? Taking multimedia on the road with them in the form of presentation graphics programs. The most common way of communicating your company's products or services to a new customer is through a form of "show and tell." This is often performed with the aid of photographs, samples, brochures, and a lot of animated discussion.

As many salespeople will be the first to tell you, they're not so much selling the customer on the company as they are on themselves. Once they have established themselves as trustworthy, loyal, intelligent, and dedicated, they can move on to the finer points of whether their products are any good or not. This takes a lot of time and costs money.

If you were to take those photographs and brochures and the animated discussion of one of your best salespeople and commit it to digital storage in the form of a multimedia presentation, it would likely have two very definable benefits. The first is a simple one: You're taking the customer's attention away from the salesperson and putting it on the company, where it belongs. A well-put-together multimedia presentation will hold the customer's attention and begin the process of educating her as to how your company does business (subtext: you're creative and high-tech), what your products are like (modern and innovative), and how you do business (well).

The second benefit is that you're standardizing the sales pitch and giving it to all the salespeople simultaneously. Not only that, you are standardizing *the best* sales pitch and replicating it to the work force. In essence, what you have done is create a clone of your best salesperson and send it out into the world.

One thing to be cautious about here: You can have the best presentation in the world, but it will be totally useless if you don't close the sale. Even with high-tech, high-glitz laptops and sophisticated presentations, your salespeople will have real work to do. They still have to figure out exactly what their customer needs, and how much he's going to have to pay for it, convince him that he really does want what you have to offer, and get him to sign on the dotted line.

What will it take to bring that level of sophistication to the field? Surprisingly little. There are several brands of laptop and noteboook microcomputers available with multimedia capabilities built in, even to the point of supporting an internal CD-ROM drive. Panasonic, Texas Instruments, and Apple all have models that you can "load and go," with built-in speakers and sound cards, large hard drives, and good-quality color Liquid Crystal Display (LCD) screens for less than $3,500 each. With one of these tucked securely under one arm your salespeople will have the ability to do multimedia whenever they smell a sale.

How about when your salespeople are in the office? Many of the aspects of networked multimedia, especially at the high end, continue to be applicable to the sales staff. Video e-mail is an excellent example. You probably didn't hire that smooth-talking sales manager for her typing skills, did you? Can you imagine how much more persuasive and effective she would be if she were communicating with her co-workers through video-enabled e-mail? And how much less time it would take for her to actually do that communicating?

If you take this concept to its logical extreme, videoconferencing is a natural for salespeople. Here's another example for you. You have a salesperson at the Chicago office who knows everything there is to know about widgets. He's also a great talker and comes across much more effectively in person than he does on the phone or in print.

At the same time you have a prospective customer in Atlanta who needs widgets. In fact, he needs *your* widgets but he just doesn't know it yet. The salesperson you have assigned to this customer in Atlanta is good, but doesn't really know the widget business. What do you do? The easy, efficient answer is that you invite the customer to your modern, spacious office in Atlanta to participate in a videoconference with the salesperson in Chicago. If you have multipoint videoconferencing, you'll bring in the product manager in Kansas City and the technical support manager in New York. That sale will likely be closed by the time everyone says "Good Morning" to each other because your company has demonstrated its technological superiority and ability to manage resources effectively.

You'll want to keep your salespeople away from sound-enabled e-mail. Remember that sound files are usually not compressed when stored and the longer the message, the larger the file, starting at big and going to gargantuan. Now add in the salesperson's natural propensity for gab and you'll see that this is a recipe for network storage disaster.

Other multimedia tools that are likely to be of benefit to salespeople include the lowly whiteboarding application, which lets any number of people sit at their own computers and "brainstorm" concepts together without the time and expense of travel. For new marketing program development or collaboration on bids, this can be a really important tool.

Speaking of bids, does the term "groupware" sound familiar? Groupware is so ideal to this kind of work that you have to wonder if it was created specifically with sales, bids, and proposals in mind. In sales, as in any other specialty, the larger the project the more people are likely to work on it.

With lots of people working on a project, especially one that means revenue (revenue = money: stuff that lets you do all these neat projects), the need to closely coordinate your company's activities and how it presents itself to the customer is of overwhelming importance. You don't want one person saying "yes" to the customer, another saying "maybe," and a third saying "sorry, no," especially when all three may be talking about the same thing.

Groupware lets everyone involved with the project know everything about that project, so communications breakdowns like that don't occur. It allows you to assign and parcel out tasks to project members, and to coordinate the completion of those tasks back into a cohesive whole. In sales image is everything, and groupware helps your company maintain a consistent image in the outside world.

CTI is of so much benefit to telemarketers (remember that inbound sales force shackled to the phones?) that it's almost a necessity. These people live and die by the telephone, and any steps that you can take to make their telephone utilization more productive pays big dollars almost immediately.

Advanced marketing systems incorporating CTI and specialized software are available that provide the ability to present marketing "scripts" and do predictive dialing (dialing at times when the callee is likely to be near the phone) that keeps the marketers busy. Most important for management, this software produces reports that tell you which employees are bringing home the bacon and which are living off the fat of the land.

FINANCE

Are you a "numbers" person or a "words" person? If you're a "words" type, you're much more comfortable visualizing objects than you are relationships. Anything that helps you do that will improve your ability to assimilate and retain information.

If you're a "numbers" type, seeing or hearing mere objects (or people) won't have nearly as much value to you. That's why networked multimedia is of extremely limited value to the folks up in the Finance or Accounting department. They are pure and simple "numbers" people, or they would not have picked the careers that they did.

If they're not going to take much value from networked multimedia, which parts are going to help them do their jobs? The answer is a simple one: whiteboarding.

One thing that happens frequently in large companies is that they are broken up by function into smaller operating units for more efficient management. They're still part of the overall operation, but they're treated like (and may actually be) independent companies. When you do that, you introduce a new word to the lexicon: *consolidations*. What it means to you and me and what it means to the accounting types are normally two separate things.

Consolidation is the act of taking information from multiple sources at a lower level and "rolling them up" to form summarized information at a higher level. An example would be a company with three divisions that each have their own profit and loss statements, which are consolidated to create a enterprise-wide profit and loss statement.

This is easy when you're talking about information that's already present in the system, like accounting records. Often the consolidation function is built right into the software, and producing consolidated statements is as easy as pushing a button. But what about when you're actively creating this information?

Finance people have two major functions: *tracking* financial activity and *forecasting* future results. The whiteboarding application can be a handy tool for getting people together to create forecasts across multiple divisions. By working together they can see the relationships between multiple data sets which help them do their job more efficiently and productively.

Other multimedia applications, like sound- and video-enabled e-mail and videoconferencing, will be appreciated by these folks, but they usually won't take the same level of value from it as other people in the company do. They make their living communicating numbers to people in and out of the organization, so seeing their smiling faces on a screen may be welcome but it won't be necessary.

Groupware is another good example of a collaborative technology that Finance usually won't be able to take full advantage of. That's because accounting applications on the network are really a form of groupware already. The data entry people in each group collaborate to enter information into the system, managers collaborate to ensure that the information is valid and current, and the controller takes the end result and produces financial statements.

Even though it's not what we would traditionally call groupware, this is really what groupware is all about—many people in many specialties working together to create a finished product.

Please realize that this is a necessary stereotyping of those poor, beleaguered "bean counters," and that not everyone will fit so neatly into this category. Realistically, though, enough of them do to make this a pretty valid set of assumptions.

Multimedia presentation graphics may have some value to the Finance squad. One of the responsibilities that the accounting group has to the rest of the company is to communicate the results of financial performance so that employees and departments know whether their performance is helping or hindering the company's growth. This information is typically disseminated in one of two forms: dull, dry spreadsheets and graphs, or dull dry presentations using overhead projections of spreadsheets and graphs.

Adding multimedia aspects to these presentations may not make the numbers work any better, but they'll probably look a lot better. Creative use of color, fonts, and transitions can spice up any presentation, even one of these, but you should remember that in this situation there are aspects of multimedia that are better left alone. For example, it would be inappropriate to have the sound board playing *The 1812 Overture* when announcing lackluster sales results, or Beethoven's *Pastoral Symphony* when making the case for layoffs or restructuring.

Likewise, animation or video may add an aura of excessive cuteness to what should be a serious and focused discussion.

RESEARCH AND DEVELOPMENT

We'll have to stereotype a bit more here as well. As with Finance, our assumptions won't fit everyone but they will fit enough to make this a worthwhile exercise.

R&D people are often a bit of a contradiction in terms. They're visionaries and creative types who never take anything for granted and are constantly looking for better methods and materials to use in their quest for excellence. At the same time they're often detail-oriented engineering types who aren't comfortable with something until they have disassembled it and reassembled it, and can explain to the nth degree how it works.

Obviously, whiteboarding is going to be a very useful tool for these folks. The ability to come together and brainstorm over a document or drawing that provides them with a valuable tool for creating and refining products or processes can pay for itself very quickly.

Groupware will have significant benefits for the same reasons. The ability to use a centralized system for project administration and idea sharing is one that has obvious benefits to this part of the business. In fact, it may have even greater benefit than you might think.

Research and Development people are creative types. They're deductive reasoners but intuitive creators. A lot of them (enough of them that even this stereotype is valid) are terrific at managing multimillion-dollar projects inside their own heads, but can't manage to keep their desks clean. Groupware offers the opportunity to let the system itself keep administrative chaos at bay.

Other multimedia applications will have a great deal of value as well, but for less objective reasons. Research and Development people are by and large technology junkies, always looking for their next jolt of computer excitement. New processors, fast hard drives, and sexy programs are intoxicating to them, and they respond extremely well to the introduction of new tools for doing their work.

Sound- and video-enabled electronic mail is a perfect example of late-generation applications to be embraced and used, although perhaps not for their intended purposes. Videoconferencing will likewise be a sought-after toy to play with.

Multimedia presentation graphics straddles the line between useful application and toy. Once the ideas have been finalized there will be a need to communicate them to management and the rest of the organization. Using the animation techniques present in late-generation presentation software to show what you mean can be beneficial, especially if the concept is complex or novel.

Good use of color and movement for slide to slide can add to the value of the presentation, as can a muted and appropriate soundtrack. Try to avoid garish color combinations, loud rock and roll riffs, and jarring transitions.

Regardless of the intended uses, what R&D people use these things for doesn't really matter. As long as they're happy, they'll be productive at their real jobs, and that's the result we're interested in.

HUMAN RESOURCES

What used to be called the "Employment Office" now has a loftier title. This is partly because of the prevailing atmosphere of "political correctness" (PC as opposed to the PC of "Personal Computer"— the one you are, the other you use). The other major reason that personnel people are now called Human Resources (HR) has a lot to do with government regulation.

It used to be that being an employer was a simple business. You had employees, so you paid them and gave them some simple benefits to keep them happy and to attract new employees competitively. If your business was unionized, you had the the added responsibility of arguing about how much to pay them and how happy to keep them, and that was about it.

Nowadays that is definitely *not* "about it." There are taxes, reporting requirements, contracts with "prevailing wage" conditions, hiring, firing, Equal Opportunity Employer (EOE) and Affirmative Action requirements, employee counseling, unemployment, disability and health insurance program administration, and many additional smaller responsibilities.

One thing to be remembered as you go through this process is that Human Resources is going to be a very strong advocate of practically every networked multimedia application you choose to implement, simply because it is going to benefit from it directly. The only exception to this is whiteboarding, which in most companies is (paradoxically) too simple for HR to take effective advantage of within its own department.

The exception to the exception (still with me?) would be extremely large companies with distributed HR departments. If that's your company, all bets are off because they'll take everything you have to offer.

Those are the *direct* benefits. Every single networked multimedia technology also has *indirect* benefits to HR because it has benefits to the company. Any technology or process that improves the lot of the workers is going to be of interest to HR because a happy, productive workforce is its stock in trade.

Whiteboarding, the only application with limited utility within the HR department, has great value outside that department. Using whiteboarding for training and interactive idea sessions is a great idea as far as HR is concerned, even if its people are not the ones being trained or brainstormed.

As for directly applicable technologies, it's a veritable smorgasbord. Sound and video e-mail get the word out quickly, efficiently, and personally. It should be no surprise the Human Resources will appreciate the human touch, so voice and video will be clear winners as far as it's concerned.

Groupware will likewise be looked upon with favor, especially as it has the potential to link this department even more closely to projects and proposals for the purposes of monitoring government requirements, employment levels and scheduling concerns.

HR will *love* multimedia presentation graphics. A big part of the HR administrator's responsibility is explaining company benefit programs to employees, and many of these benefits can be difficult to explain. How do you get a recent high school graduate working on the shop floor to recognize the value of retirement planning and the 401(k) plan? By using lots of color, graphics, and flashy examples that catch her attention.

Sound has great value here, providing an opportunity for you to be more creative than you can be with other types of presentations. Jazz, rock and roll, world beat, and other styles are all appropriate methods for jazzing up (pardon the pun) presentations.

Animation can be used to great effect as well. Why lay on a series of graphs showing how your retirement money will grow in the 401(k) when you can show a single graph with that little green line inching its way to the top? The HR people might even choose to inject a little humor by having the top of the graph explode or by making a small door open in the top as the line reaches it. With good multimedia presentation software and a creative designer, the sky may not be the limit after all.

CTI is another application that has benefit to HR because it benefits its clients, the employees.

Videoconferencing will be of limited benefit within the department (if it has any benefit at all), but will be appreciated and used by others, including executive management who may well use it to talk to the upper-level people in HR.

PRODUCTION

This category really deals with production management personnel. For networked multimedia applications for actual production workers, take a look at "The Rank and File" section below.

Production management people are going to be concerned mostly with operational issues, so interactive multimedia won't be a very high priority for them. In fact, it may even be viewed as an unwanted distraction from their day-to-day job of making sure that the widgets get built. Whiteboarding and videoconferencing are likely to be viewed with suspicion or outright hatred.

So what *does* grab these people's attention? Things that make it easier for them to do their job, and in this case that means sound- and video-enabled electronic mail and groupware. Audio e-mail allows them to obtain the information they need without having to wade through a lot of documents to get to it; and more important, it allows them to send messages to other people without having to sit down at the computer and type a lot of text. After all, if that was what they wanted to do they'd be in Accounting, right?

Video e-mail has the same attractions. Production managers are people persons, used to interacting with subordinates and superiors face to face but usually on their own terms and schedule. Using video e-mail to extend that capability throughout the company definitely has its attractions.

Groupware follows right along with this, too. The more closely production is coordinated with the rest of the company, the happier everyone is. Do Sales' forecasts project a 30-percent increase over the next quarter? Production needs to start planning for overtime or increased hiring now. Does R&D have a trendy new product coming to the manufacturing floor? Production needs to think about how to schedule while continuing to make the products the company already makes.

Groupware can also be very useful in distributed organizations with more than one production facility. Using this application allows managers to share notes with each other in the same fashion as in electronic mail but with a much smoother and easier path when it comes to soliciting comments and suggestions from their peers. Rather than a long round-robin of e-mail notes from each participant to all the others being used, a single collaborative document can serve as the platform for constructive discussion and planning.

You can leave the multimedia presentation graphics in the box for this gang. They don't need it, they don't want it, and if you try to give it to them, they'll give it right back.

THE RANK AND FILE

It's difficult to generalize in this area, as every business is unique, especially when it comes to the people who do the everyday things that keep the business running. Even though there are as many ways of doing business as there are businesses, there are certain constants for every organization. We'll look at the areas where there appears to be some commonality and draw at least a few conclusions.

The larger the business is, the more likely that people who do real work will be isolated from people who make decisions about what sort of work they do. This is not a good thing, and the larger the company, the harder it is to overcome this.

Networked multimedia offers a few opportunities to overcome this gap, at least as far as the people who use computers are concerned. Sound- and video-enabled e-mail leaps to mind as a possible conduit for maintaining a more substantial connection between the executive suite and the production floor.

Take the concept of a company newsletter as an example. While printed media can be effective for getting the word out, it is a highly impersonal manner of doing so. Often, the newsletter arrives anonymously along with a carton of other intracompany materials, and the recipients don't even have the satisfaction of having it addressed to them personally.

Now contrast that with using e-mail as the delivery medium. A voice e-mail recorded by a company officer or other muckety-muck conveys the same information, but it comes, literally, "right from the horse's mouth." A video e-mail has an even greater effect. Not only are you receiving the information directly from the source, but now she can look you in the eye as she does it.

The overhead cost of delivering this technology to the rank and file can be minimal. A really basic PC doesn't even have to have the sound card installed, as there are drivers available for free that use the PC's speaker for audio output. The quality stinks (to put it mildly), but it can be done and there is no cost associated with doing it.

Do frontline personnel need the ability to generate sounds and images? In most cases the answer will be no. One exception is the company that has people doing similar things in disparate locations. Offering these folks the ability to communicate on something more sophisticated than a simple phone call can pay for itself in increased efficiency and, more important, a reduction in duplicated mistakes. If this is the case, whiteboarding will definitely be on the shopping list.

Groupware doesn't seem to have any attraction or benefit at this level, but every company is different. Yours may very well be organized in such a fashion that there's a place for groupware, so evaluate it as carefully as you do other technologies. Just don't be surprised if the answer is no.

On the other hand, multimedia presentation graphics will almost certainly be a resounding yes, but only for the people who are the recipients of this application within the business. Every department that needs to communicate to the frontline elements of the business would do well to leverage this program to make its presentations more effective and easier to understand, especially Human Resources.

Sound-enabled e-mail can be valuable if you don't already offer its less flashy cousin, voice mail. Video e-mail probably won't be an option because of the cost per station, and on-line videoconferencing will almost certainly be out.

CUSTOMERS AND VENDORS

M any times we judge the value of a technology solely by its effect within the business unit alone, but nowadays that vision can be dangerously shortsighted. Leveraging what you have internally can bring you new business, keep or enhance existing business, and offer cost and productivity savings when you extend them beyond the enterprise.

Like moths to a flame, customers can be attracted to the bright light of your technological vision regardless of the business you're in. Vendors likewise enjoy working with customers who know what they want and take strides to ensure that they get exactly that.

Many late-generation applications can be successfully extended beyond the boundaries of your office into the offices of your customers and vendors. What this will require is an extension of the network itself out into the big wide world. If you read through Chapter 4 and said, "Nice stuff, but it's not for me," perhaps you might want to read this chapter and then go back and take another look with these thoughts in mind.

Customers

How do you get a new customer? Those of you who immediately responded with "bribery" may now pack your belongings and head for a small South American country. The rest of us attract customers by offering them more value, lower prices, or both.

How do you keep a customer? Those of you who answered "blackmail" may go join the others down south of the equator. Again, those of us who are left know that we keep customers by making sure that they remain happy with our services, our product, or our personnel.

The process of attracting a customer to your business instead of to someone else's is called differentiation. If you can prove conclusively that you are bigger, better, stronger, or faster than the guy down the block, you are likely to win the business. Networked multimedia offers you the opportunity to use technology as a differentiator and as a facilitator.

One major factor in today's business environment is the ability to be responsive to your customers' needs. Their needs will change as their customers' needs change, and their customers' needs, ad infinitum. Can you be more responsive than your competitors? Yes.

We've already talked about the benefits of multimedia presentation graphics in the "Sales and Marketing" section of this chapter. It's good. It's really, really good, and you should do it. 'Nuff said.

There a lot of additional opportunities to be examined as well. Take the lowly whiteboarding application as an example. It works almost equally well on dial-up lines as it does on the network. What better way to show your customers that you're serious about understanding their needs than to install the application and a modem on one of their computers? Now you can have teleconferences where presentations are made remotely, documents can be prepared and collaborated on interactively, and new processes and products can be hashed out together. With this level of integration you are offering to make them partners rather than simply customers.

Groupware can extend this philosophy even further, making the concept of collaborative computing a truly global one. Be careful, though. Once you offer customers this level of integration, security becomes a definite concern. It's all very well to offer them tight integration between your plans and theirs, but don't offer them tight integration between your plans, theirs, and those of their competitors. Loose lips sink ships, especially in these litigious times.

Is a particular company a really important customer? Do you have a lot of interaction with it? Why not extend the network right into its facility? With low-cost ISDN circuits and routers, you can add one or more PCs that are tied directly into your LAN and share the benefits of sound- and video-enabled e-mail with your customers.

Remember that the further away they are, the more valuable this approach is. It can be tiresome and tedious to track down a salesperson or customer representative when you are separated by two, three, or more time zones. "First thing in the morning" for them could be lunchtime or later for you.

Adding videoconferencing is a possibility, but the cost will likely be prohibitive for a few years yet. High-quality video will require ISDN Primary Rate at around $500 a month just for the access. Add a capital investment of $8,000 to $10,000 for the PC with video equipment, and you see that this has to be a very good customer to justify the expense. Besides, if you're fighting a time zone difference, you or the customer could end up talking to empty chairs a lot of the time.

Vendors

On the other side of the equation are the people who do things for you. Your vendors may not be as technologically advanced as you are, so why wait? All of the benefits that you could give your customers could also accrue to you as the customer. Whiteboards and sound and video e-mail all add value to the relationship and can be valuable in other ways as well.

There are many ways that networked multimedia can be used to leverage your relationship with a major vendor. For example, using the whiteboarding application cooperatively to design new products or subassemblies with their knowledge and input may save you from missteps or miscalculations that could cost time and dollars.

Groupware adds to this concept and enhances it. Your vendor doesn't have to wait for a whiteboard conference to get its two cents in. If you assume that you are going to implement groupware, then adding the vendor to the interactive design and planning process will cost very little and pay benefits far in excess of the associated costs. Remember, it takes only one prevented mistake to save thousands or even millions of dollars, so this is cheap insurance indeed.

Remember the security aspect. It would not do to tell your vendor too much and have it offering access to technologies your company has developed that may not be trademarked or patented yet. You may be able to prove that the vendor let the cat out of the bag, but by that time the cat is either a long way down the street or has been hit by one of your competitor's semitrailers, if you'll excuse the metaphor.

Do multimedia presentation graphics hold any special benefit here? To be honest, not really. On an external basis you don't really have to use color to sell the vendor on your company, just on the color of your money. If Research and Development is using this application to display new technologies internally, it may very well be desirable to use those same presentations to illustrate to vendors what's really going on. Even so, it would be difficult to think of a single instance where custom presentations would need to be prepared for vendors alone.

Giving your vendor sound-enabled e-mail access would be more of a perk than anything else, as there isn't a lot of value to add by moving from text e-mail delivered by a common carrier or the Internet, to voice-enabled mail, because that's really how the voice mail you probably already have on your telephone system works.

Adding video-enabled e-mail may be a whole different kettle of fish. Let's say that a vendor's production manager is having trouble getting one of your part designs through manufacturing. Rather than make elaborate (and perhaps incorrect or misleading) references to the part that is causing the trouble, think how much more effective it would be to have that person sit before the camera and visually indicate the errant calculations!

What is it worth to your vendors to have you integrate your operations with theirs? Your initiative makes them more flexible, more responsive, and more profitable. That should translate into real dollar savings for you when it comes time to tote the tab.

In the most extreme case they may really like what you've done and want to do it for their other customers, or for their vendors. If those customers aren't your competitors, there may be some consulting income for you or your company.

If they're not interested, they should be. It's really in both of your best interests to develop the technological level of your interconnection as far as possible, simply because it promises to add efficiency and save costs on both sides of the modem. In fact, the potential gains are so strong that if your current vendors are resistant to automating your interactions with them, you should consider looking for other vendors who aren't quite so resistant, or, at a minimum, using the threat of going looking to get your current vendors to reconsider their position.

What Benefits Does the Organization Reap?

On an internal basis the organization is poised to collect some intangible benefits and quite a few tangible ones. Providing an exact measurement of benefits received both before and after the fact may prove problematic, but that's a common complaint and not just for technology-related gains.

Employee morale will definitely improve. You are adding value to all jobs that the new stuff touches, without requiring any significant amount of new knowledge or retraining. Employees will be better informed, more comfortable about their roles in the organization, and more willing to communicate with their peers. In this environment productivity has to improve, and depending on the department and job function, that improvement should be measurable.

Will the improvements justify the cost of attaining them? In a word, yes. You're making a one-time investment (a capital investment at that, which is infinitely preferable to an expense. Just ask your Accounting department). That investment will translate into reduced labor, telephone, copying, printing and fax expense. On a dollars-spent-for-dollars-saved basis, you will almost certainly recover the cost of the equipment within its depreciable life. Here's a simple example.

Assume that you have a network with 50 workstations, and you wish to add whiteboarding and sound-enabled e-mail to all 50. You calculate that you will never have more than four simultaneous whiteboarding sessions with five participants each, so you'll need a 20-user license for the whiteboarding software.

Additionally, assume that each use of the whiteboarding software saves the person using it a half-hour of time in setting up, getting to, and returning from a meeting, and that there are, on average, 100 uses of the software each month, which is conservative. Also assume that each use of sound-enabled e-mail saves a $.25 phone call and that there are 20 uses of sound-enabled e-mail per business day. As icing on the cake, assume that having all this tasty stuff creates a 2 percent gain in overall employee productivity, which is similarly conservative.

We'll use a labor cost of $15 per hour to perform our calculations. Here's how it breaks out:

Costs:

Whiteboarding software	$ 4,000
Sound boards @ $100 each (good ones)	5,000
Speakers @ $20/pair (okay ones)	1,000
Microphones @ $10/each (okay ones)	500
Sound-enabling software for e-mail	0
Total	$10,500

Benefits:

Whiteboarding @ 50 hours saved per month	$	750
Sound enabled e-mail @ 400 uses per month		100
Overall productivity gains @ $2/day/employee		2,000
Total		**$ 2,850/month**

The payback in real dollars is as little as four months!

On an external basis it's close to impossible for me to estimate just how much you'll make or save using networked multimedia with your customers and vendors, but you should be able to come up with some hard numbers.

How much more will your customers order when they can do so more easily? How much time and energy will be saved when you have to respond to changes in schedules or designs? Only you will be able to answer these questions, but the odds are very strong that the numbers will be significant.

With vendors it can be easy to estimate savings because you can simply demand them. Offer vendors all the features that you want to see from your site to theirs, and then demand appropriate adjustments to their pricing and/or terms. Will they be willing to do this? If you show them how much money and time they can save, you'd better believe they will.

Just by implementing these two technologies you're going to be able to show solid, sizable gains in efficiency and productivity. Cost savings should be as easily apparent. What may not be quite as apparent is that you've laid the foundation for several other networked multimedia applications, so costs of implementation for follow-on projects will be quite a bit lower than before. In other words, you're on a roll. Go for it.

6 IMPLEMENTATION STRATEGIES

So, you want to do this networked multimedia thing, do you? The only problem is that your network is of typical 80s construction and now you want to support 90s applications. Don't worry, this chapter will give you the road map to successful implementation. And all it's going to cost is money and time.

GETTING FROM HERE TO THERE

If you have a mainstream network today, what you probably have is a mixed bag of personal computers. About half are two to three years old, are based on the Intel 386 chip, and run at 33 Mhz or less. The remainder are Intel 486 based, mostly at 33 Mhz, but you'll have a few 486DX2/66 machines that you bought in the last six months or so. The network topology is Ethernet 10BaseT, and you're running it over Category 3 cable.

In all probability you're using Novell NetWare version 3.12 as the network operating system, but a few of you avant garde types will have Microsoft Lan Manager or one of the several peer-to-peer network operating systems.

On the workstations it's a mixed bag of DOS and Windows software. Your people all want the latest and greatest, and you're constantly having to tell them that they cannot have the software they want or warning them that it's going to be too slow for their tastes.

Okay, that's today. We want to get to that magical, mystical tomorrow where data, voice, and video all fly about the network with equal ease and speed. How do we do this? By thinking big but starting small.

If you're going to build a state-of-the-art multimedia-enabled network, there are two ways to do it. The first way is to throw everything you have now into the trash can and take out a loan for a million dollars. Immediately after that decide that the job will be too hard and buy yourself a plane ticket to the Netherlands Antilles, where you can be a rich but technologically challenged individual. No, wait, that's not right.

Seriously, you take that million clams and build a new network from the ground up. Category 5 cable or, even better, fiber optic to the desktop; no computer slower than a Pentium/90; MPEG CODECS in every box; video cameras perched jauntily atop the 21-inch monitors, and the best, most comprehensive and expensive software available.

Can you do that? I thought not. As with everything else on the network, if you want to get to state-of-the-art, you're going to have to do it through the mainstream, which brings us to the second way to get there from here.

The best way to bring your network to full multimedia capability is to divide the tasks into hardware and software. On the hardware side start at the workstations and work your way in to the server. On the software side start at the server and work your way out.

WORKSTATION UPGRADES

You need to realize now that most of the personal computers you have are not going to be around when you get to the end of the rainbow. If you have any 286 PCs left in the business at all, you're already thinking about getting rid of them just to be able to run nonmultimedia applications.

386-class PCs just can't handle the throughput necessary for multimedia, but there's no reason to make folks suffer while they're waiting for the best and the brightest to land on their desks. Therefore, you need to look at what you can do to make their lives more comfortable in the interim.

Math Coprocessors and Processor Upgrades

If that older PC is being used for Windows, one thing you can do for your users quickly and cheaply is to slap a math coprocessor into the box. A math coprocessor slips into a slot somewhere in the general vicinity of the main processor and once installed tells the math portion of the main processor to "Go to sleep. I'll handle things from now on."

Regular processors have the ability to do simple math only, at least as far as the hardware is concerned. If there's fancy math involved (like manipulating graphical images), the processor has to perform those operations by combining lots of simpler ones. This takes time in the form of processor cycles and slows down the whole machine significantly.

Math coprocessors have hundreds of these fancy math operations stored in their hardware, so they zip through graphics and other large number-crunching operations. Installing a math coprocessor in a 386-class PC will yield up to a sixfold speed increase under certain circumstances, and the math chips cost as little as $25 each. That's a very small price to pay for such a big jump up in power.

Microcomputers of the 486DX-class already have the math coprocessor built in, so a low-cost speed bump just isn't available here. Unfortunately, 486SX-class machines are in even worse shape. A 486SX chip is really a 486DX with the math coprocessor and another part called the cache carved out.

In order to upgrade you have two choices, and neither of them is very pretty. If the machine supports it, you can remove the SX chip and replace it with a DX at a cost of around $150. Alternatively, you can purchase and install an Intel "Overdrive" chip.

The Overdrive processor is really a full-fledged 486DX with an extra pin sticking out of the bottom. This chip literally turns off the original SX processor. You could install an Overdrive chip and then yank the SX chip out of the computer, and it wouldn't even notice. Overdrive chips cost from $200 to $350 each, depending on the speed of the main board, so this is not a very cost-effective way to achieve better performance.

Under other circumstances processor upgrades *can* be an inexpensive way to upgrade your computer's overall performance. There are different types and styles of processor upgrade, depending on the original processor installed.

Computers with the Intel 80386SX usually have the processor glued to the main board, so you can't remove the old processor and pop in a new one. What you'll do instead is install a processor that snaps right over the top of the existing one and "piggybacks" on it. These on-top processors literally turn off the chip underneath them and perform all the computer's processing after that.

This particular upgrade type gets you a lot of bang for your buck. The upgrade processors are usually "clock-doubled," which means that they operate at twice the speed of the processor they replace. A 20-Mhz machine instantly becomes a pseudo-40 Mhz, a 25-Mhz becomes a pseudo-50, and so on. Because the main board continues to operate at the slower speed, you don't get all the benefits of the faster processor but you do get a really big boost in computational speed.

Most 80386SX-based computers have this option available, but not all. Unfortunately, the oldest 80386SX chips operating at 16 Mhz are not upgradeable, as only the chips manufactured during the last six months at that particular speed have the "cut out pin" that allows you to install an upgrade processor.

There's no easy way to tell whether yours is an "early" or "late" processor, so it's probably better simply to assume that SX-16s aren't upgradeable. There are snap-on upgrade processors available for all 80386SX 20-, 25-, and 33-Mhz speeds.

The processor chip in 80386DX computers is a standard one with a whole bunch of pins sticking out of the bottom. When you purchase an upgrade processor it usually comes with a metal or plastic tool for removing the old one. Once the chip is removed, hang on to it until you know the new one is working; then you can toss it out. Alternatively, see if your local computer parts shop will give you a couple of bucks for it to be used as a spare part or melted down for the gold on the pins. They also make great jewelry.

80386DX processors are usually upgraded to a special version of the 486SX that sits in the same socket the old processor did. These 386/486SX chips are also normally clock-doubled and can give that older machine quite a boost. Since they're SX, you don't get the math coprocessor capability unless you pay for it separately.

Computers with 486DX processors can be upgraded to newer, faster 486DX chips, or they may have a big flat socket called a "ZIF" (Zero Insertion Force) next to the processor for a Pentium Overdrive processor.

If you're a forward-thinking type, even the Pentium you bought last week will be upgradeable sometime next year when Intel ships the "P6" processor.

Did you buy an Apple Macintosh? These machines can be upgraded, too. It's called a "trade in program," and this is how it works. You bring your Macintosh to the dealer. He gives you a fraction of what it's worth. You buy a whole new Macintosh or PowerPC. You go home.

RAM Cram

Does that PC have four or fewer megabytes of RAM? Bring it up to eight megabytes and watch the look of delight on your user's face. There is a commonly described "sweet spot" for performance under Windows at the 8-megabyte point. Less than that causes lots of swaps and pauses, and more goes largely unutilized.

When you add that memory look for late-generation Windows programs like Microsoft Word for Windows, or Excel and Novell's WordPerfect for Windows to take a *huge* jump up in performance, especially as far as the user interface is concerned. Screens update more quickly, menus can be accessed more readily, users can switch between programs almost instantaneously, and almost everything about the computer gets immediately and measurably better. At around $150 per four megabytes of RAM, an upgrade here can pay for itself in increased productivity very quickly.

You'll have to get used to the idea of needing ever-increasing amounts of RAM, especially if you're going to be moving to next-generation operating systems like Windows 95. Win95 works a little slower than Windows 3.1 with four megabytes of RAM, speeds up quite a bit with eight, and continues to improve with each successive memory installation. The "sweet spot" doesn't appear to exist anymore.

Windows 3.1 manages memory by dividing it up into 64,000-byte segments. Running multiple programs at the same time means that Windows keeps moving these segments around, and at some point it starts to spend more time moving segments than it does running programs. That's why it appears efficient at 8 megabytes but only slightly more efficient at 16. You've doubled the number of segments to be managed.

Windows 95 uses a 32-bit linear addressing method that treats all of RAM as one big flat space. The more RAM you have, the bigger the space is, and the more programs that can be stuffed into it without incurring a systems overhead penalty.

Making It Sing

Even if that computer isn't going to be around when the network is completed, go ahead and add a sound board, speakers (or a headset), and a microphone when you can afford to do so. Next-generation computers, regardless of the expansion bus type used, will still support the older ISA adapters, and you won't need a lot of throughput to support sound alone. Buy that new PC and move the sound board into it when the existing computer is replaced.

Having sound capability means that your users can begin to experiment with and hopefully make good use of sound enabled e-mail immediately. We'll discuss this in more detail on the software side, but it's likely that there won't be any additional cost associated with this upgrade other than the cost of the parts and installing them.

One major consideration: Don't buy an 8-bit sound board regardless of how inexpensive it is. Get a 16-bit board, because 8-bit boards don't have enough resistance to electromagnetic interference in newer, higher-speed computers. This translates into an unacceptable amount of noise, which manifests itself as a loud hiss during recording and playback. If the recording already has a lot of hiss and you play it back on a computer that injects still more, the result can be completely unintelligible.

Faster Video

Graphical operating environments like Windows and OS/2 place very heavy demands on the computer's video controller circuitry. You can often make an older, slower machine behave like a young punk by exchanging the old video controller for a newer design.

Old video cards rely on the main processor to manipulate video memory and the display. If the processor is already taxed by applications in use, it will slow down operation of the computer by quite a bit.

Newer video cards work around the processor bottleneck in one of several ways. If your computer has the ISA bus only, an accelerated card with its own graphics processor takes a huge load off the main processor as soon as the accelerator is installed. If your computer has VL-BUS or PCI, not only does the video card relieve the processor of manipulating images, but it also takes charge of moving video information into and out of RAM. In essence your computer becomes a true multiprocessor machine, and the performance improvement is impressive.

Remember to verify that the new video card has a fully functional feature connector for later video e-mail and videoconferencing upgrades. You might even want to consider getting one of the new breed of accelerated video cards with built-in video capture/playback and MPEG capability. Essentially you're adding the ability to make that station do certain types of low-end videoconferencing along with the ability to play back stored video in full-screen mode, right along with the basic display capability.

Since this is a new offering it is anything but cheap, but prices are likely to fall quite rapidly. Several Taiwanese manufacturers have already brought variants of this board type to market, with street prices as low as $350 each. This translates to double or triple the cost of a good accelerated VGA adapter but less than the cost of a VGA adapter and MPEG player if purchased separately.

It would be wise to hold off purchasing video equipment until you're ready to take the big plunge. While this equipment will work acceptably on older equipment, it won't work well, again because of a lack of available speed on the expansion bus. This time the culprit is going to be the video adapter. Providing full-motion video at 30 frames per second on a viewing window larger than a postage stamp is just too much for those old boxes, so it's better to wait until you begin to put the newer, speedier stuff in.

CD-ROM

If a user has a definite and immediate need, you can add a CD-ROM directly to her computer, but try not to do so. It's much more cost-effective to provide shared CD-ROM at the server or on dedicated servers.

The user should have to prove to you that she uses a variety of CD-ROMs on a daily basis, that she is the only person likely to use them (otherwise you're on the hook to purchase multiple copies) and that it would be difficult and time consuming for her to run over to the server every time she needs to change out a disk.

Network Adapters

Your choices are extremely limited here. Unless you have Pentium-based computers on the network, you're going to be limited to ISA-based network adapters at 10 megabits per second for Ethernet and 16 megabits per second for Token Ring. Faster network topologies will not be available to 386- and 486-class computers because either the expansion bus just isn't fast enough to handle the throughput or, like VL-BUS, it's too unstable to use effectively. It's better to buy the least expensive adapter for your topology and be prepared to throw it away when it's time to replace the computer.

If you already have Pentium-based computers, take a look at the section "New Computer Purchases" below. For network adapters the advice is the same.

What Do I Do with the Old Stuff?

One alternative to pitching old equipment in the trash is to donate it to your local public school or community college. Schools are never at the leading edge when it comes to equipment, and because of budget constraints they are often quite a way behind the mainstream.

Your donation of used equipment will be entirely appropriate, greatly appreciated, and fully tax deductible. Even if they can't use it, they may be able to sell it to someone and use the money for operating funds. In any case, when you do this everyone wins.

New Computer Purchases

Repeat after me: "I buy PCI." Intel's Peripheral Component Interconnect is going to be the dominant expansion bus structure for the remainder of the decade. All Pentium-based systems now come with at least three PCI expansion slots, and late word is that Intel's next-generation processor, called "P6" at press time, will have two separate PCI buses in it for maximum throughput.

With PCI in your boxes, you'll be able to handle several millions of bytes per second of throughput. Whether you base your network on Fast Ethernet, 100VG-AnyLAN, ATM, or any other emerging technology, PCI will handle them all.

With regard to the processor, the faster the better. Don't break the bank, because there will be lots of other components to purchase, but get the most processing bang for your buck that you can. The Pentium/90 is a good low-end processor.

For the network adapter consider Fast Ethernet (100BaseTX) as favorably as you can. All current adapters work at both the current 10 megabits per second of standard Ethernet and at the 100 megabits per second of Fast Ethernet. This allows you to add computers to your existing network without major expansion; then, when you are ready to support the faster speed, you simply reconfigure the adapter, preserving your investment.

When you're ready to increase the network speed, you'll upgrade the server to faster adapters, replace your old 10BaseT hubs with new ones, reconfigure the adapters, and you're on your way.

100BaseVG-AnyLAN is another good alternative. It means a lot more money up front because you'll have to purchase new network hubs and upgrade your server at the beginning, but your wiring investment is preserved. Remember, under most network topologies you can mix and match faster and slower adapters by putting both kinds in the server and creating both fast and slow segments. As you replace older computers, you'll shift the replacements from one side to the other by plugging them into the new hubs.

ENHANCING THE EXISTING NETWORK

Ethernet and Token Ring: What You Can Do with Them Now

The best option available for maximizing what you have now is to split up the network into as many segments as your server can handle. If all of your workstations are on a single network segment, there's a lot of bandwidth going to waste. If you create as many individual segments as you can (usually subject to hardware limitations in the server), the amount of traffic on each segment is limited to the computers on that segment rather than all the computers everywhere (see Figure 6.1).

In this case, the server acts not only as a server but as a router, making sure that only packets that are actually destined for that part of the network go

Figure 6.1 Using segmentation to improve operating-system performance.

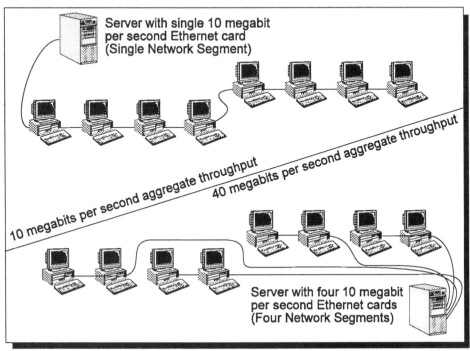

there. If you take a typical single-segment Ethernet LAN with 50 workstations and break it into four segments with around 12 workstations each, you'll see about 30-percent better network speed overall. This is important because you *can* add some multimedia-enabled applications right now, rather than wait for faster networks and newer PCs.

You can do the same thing with Token Ring, and the results will be significant but not quite as dramatic. A safe number to use is around a 20-percent speed improvement.

If your server already has EISA or PCI expansion slots, you have a very powerful option for increasing the network bandwidth. Consider adding a 100-megabit-per-second card to the server and connecting the card to a dual-speed switching hub or a router.

On the 100-Mbps side you can choose from Fast Ethernet, 100BaseVG-AnyLAN, or FDDI/CDDI. On the lower speed side you can continue to use the Ethernet or Token Ring you have now, with the added capability of getting data into or out of the server up to 10 times faster than you did before.

The most cost-effective way to accomplish this is probably going to be with Fast Ethernet in the server and Fast Ethernet 10/100 switching hubs. The switching hubs work just fine (in fact, they work terrific) with standard Ethernet cards, and if by some miracle you have workstations with PCI or EISA, you can put Fast Ethernet cards in them, too, and experience what a really fast network is like.

PLANNING FOR FASTER TOPOLOGIES

Eventually you're going to run up against the limitations of your existing network, especially with regard to the server's ability to accept, retain, and disseminate information. At that point you'll be able to go to the powers that be and ask for the funds to move to a faster network.

Unfortunately, you can't just sit still till then. Networks are not static devices like toasters or microwaves. As the company's needs change, the network must change to accommodate them. More workstations, fewer workstations, workstations in different places than they were before, and always, always the need for more and more storage capacity.

Parkinson's Third Law states: "Work expands to fill the available space." Whoever this Parkinson guy was, he hit the nail right on the head, especially when it comes to hard drives. If you purchase a 40-megabyte drive, you will shortly have 80 megabytes of data to put on it. If it's an 80, you'll end up with 160. Regardless of how much you have, just wait a few months and you'll need more.

Moves, changes, additions, and deletions can be looked at in one of three ways. The most common viewpoint is that this is "business as usual" that requires us to maintain the status quo and is simply part of our day-to-day job. A less common viewpoint is that these are irritating distractions that pull us away from the main part of our job—providing newer, better software resources to our users and enhancing network reliability.

Change Is Good

The third way is the best way to look at it. Each time something changes on the network, it's an *opportunity*. You don't have to simply take the existing stuff and shuffle it around to match what's needed. Instead, ask yourself what could be done to make this little corner of the network better than it was before, at least with regard to next-generation (read networked multimedia) capabilities.

It could be something very simple. Instead of relocating that Category 3 cable, have new Category 5 cable pulled. Make sure that the wall plates are Cat 5 as well. Take the opportunity to install that extra four megabytes of RAM, or exchange the older network card for a newer, faster one. Each baby step you take here will add up to one big leap for the network (apologies to Neil Armstrong).

If this is an addition to the network, go whole hog. The incremental cost of specifying a Pentium or later processor with a PCI bus, a sound card, and a 10/100 network adapter already installed is very small compared to the cost of replacing or retrofitting later.

One thing that will really help you in situations like this, especially when it comes to cost justifications, is the Networked Multimedia Direction Statement we'll discuss in the next chapter. If the basic concept has already been proposed and accepted, you're not going to have to fight the good fight over budget and expenditures every time you want to make things a little better.

ON THE SOFTWARE SIDE

You can add multimedia presentation graphics to the environment any old time. Since this is not truly a networked application, all that will be required will be desktop or laptop personal computers of sufficient speed and complexity to run the presentation graphics program that you choose.

Because of its extremely low demands on bandwidth, whiteboarding is one multimedia application that you can add to the network right away. Making this program available to your users is simple and straightforward, and it gives a good and immediate return on investment.

Assuming that you're ready to accept the technologic responsibility and increased capital cost of an additional server, you're ready to take a serious look at groupware as well. Most groupware packages are scaleable, so you can start small with just a few people making use of text-based document sharing and electronic mail. On an as-available basis you can continue to enhance the network by adding more users and groups until the whole company is tied in to the groupware concept.

Once that's accomplished, you can either drop your existing electronic mail system and enhance the groupware application for voice and/or video e-mail, or maintain two systems (much less desirable).

If you've added sound boards to enough PCs to make it worthwhile, you can provide sound-enabled e-mail. Remember that the sound files are quite large, so be sure that you've provided enough room on the server's hard disk for storing this kind of e-mail attachment.

Video e-mail can be done quite easily if you've already made the investment in cameras and controllers. The odds are that you haven't, however, and won't until you get those tasty new Pentium-based computers. Remember, it's considered bad form to kill old computers just to get new ones, so put that screwdriver down and quit scuffing your feet on the carpet, please.

Interactive video is out. O-U-T, out. You'll need to move to faster network technologies.

CURRENT APPLICATIONS: ESTIMATING EXISTING CAPACITY

When you look at network capacity you have to do so from two different viewpoints: where you're at now and where you'll be later. Overly simplistic perhaps, but it is important to find out how close to the edge you are *before* you start making additions.

There are also two measures of capacity that you want to pay attention to: space on your server and workstation hard drives, and network bandwidth.

Permanent Storage Space

Hard-drive capacity is the easy one, so we'll talk about it first. Regardless of how much you have you probably don't have enough. If the amount of free storage drops below a certain level (usually about 10 percent of the total drive capacity), you're flirting with disaster.

It's a good idea to keep a wide margin of safety when it comes to leaving free space on the disk. Twenty-five percent is good, but 40 percent is better. As people do their daily work and data sets fluctuate in size, one good burst of users and temporary files could run the server right out of disk space and stop it dead in its tracks. Networked Windows workstations and their swap files are notorious for this.

The correct way to remedy this problem is to buy more or larger hard drives. Let's face it, the buggers are cheap! A 2-gigabyte (that's 2 billion bytes of storage for the geekspeak-challenged among us) SCSI hard drive costs less than $1,000 nowadays. You *do* want to stay with SCSI drives. Even though you can buy IDE drives of the same capacity for less money, you're limited to a maximum of two drives using normal controllers and four drives using newer controllers.

Contrast that with SCSI,which supports seven drives *per controller* and as many controllers as you can stuff into the box. Also, those drives don't have to be hard drives. CD-ROM, Magneto-Optical, and tape backup units can all be plugged into a SCSI chain, so SCSI gives you options that IDE does not.

A side effect of adding drives may be the need for additional RAM in the network server. Novell NetWare servers in particular need a fair amount of RAM to provide buffered access to data and to give faster access to file directories.

Network Bandwidth

The other bellwether of network capacity is the network cable itself. Watch your bandwidth! Every individual component that we add to the network steals just a little bit more capacity than the component that preceded it. New versions of programs stored on the network will almost always be larger than the version they supersede.

You'll need to be vigilant about what applications you allow onto the network and how those applications are installed and utilized. For many years the general concept has been that most applications should be installed on the network server to take advantage of the "simultaneous users" clause of licenses which lets you buy only the number of copies you need to serve all the users of a program at any given time rather than the total number of users of that program.

You may very well want to reconsider this. Remember that the cost of software is likely to be the smallest component of the purchase. Installation, training, and support will likely cost several times what you shelled out in the first place, and the maintenance/upgrade cycle will continue to take dollars out of your pocket.

Once the application is comfortably installed on the server it's going to take bandwidth from your network cable, and that cumulative addition of time may have two results.

The first result might be that this application is the straw that breaks the camel's back, and your whole network will slow to an unacceptable pace. The second and far more likely scenario is that this particular application just doesn't react well to shared installation. A lot of late-generation programs are like that, especially Windows-based programs.

These programs use a relatively small executable file that allows them to load quickly, or so it seems. What really happens is that the rest of the program (and there's typically a *lot* of "rest") is contained in Dynamic Link Libraries or .DLL files. The word *library* is significant. When the program calls for a routine that's stored in the Library, the rest of the Library comes along for the ride. A megabyte or more of totally useless data may be stuffed into RAM along with the 60,000 you really needed. If that megabyte arrived across the network cable it probably (a) took too long and (b) caused everyone else to slow down momentarily.

This doesn't even begin to address the problem of programs that are too large to fit into memory all at once, Windows based or not. In order to make the whole thing run these programs use swap files that are stored . . . yep, on the network, unless you specified otherwise. Kiss a little more bandwidth good bye.

So what should you do? The rational course of action is to first evaluate whether that program is truly necessary. If it is, *seriously* consider purchasing enough copies for all your users and installing them on the local hard drive.

No local hard drives on the workstations? Buy them! four-hundred-megabyte IDE drives are down under $200 these days, a mere pittance when compared with the possible loss of employee productivity from "swap waits."

NEW APPLICATIONS: ESTIMATING THE IMPACT

How do you gauge just how much load an application is going to place on the network? Unfortunately, you can't. There are just too many variables to give a stock, one-size-fits-all answer. What you can do is use a sort of checklist that will tell you if you're heading for trouble. The more questions from the following list you answer in the affirmative, the greater the likelihood that you're going to be introducing a problem instead of a solution:

1. **Does the program reside on the network?**

   Programs that live on the network server are resource hogs. They take up space on the server's hard drive, and every time a user wants to access one it has to be retrieved from the server (there goes a bit of the server's processor capacity, however briefly) and transferred across your precious network cable just so the user can get to it.

2. **Does the program require overlays or DLLs?**

   As we've already discussed, most modern programs use this technique to keep the size of individual components small, but the total program ends up being very large. One thing that you'll need to consider as a side issue is how much RAM the users' workstations have. If it's too small, the same overlays will quite likely be called up not just once but many times during a single session with the program.

   Individual overlays are used and then overlaid themselves by other parts of the program; later they have to be called back when the user repeats an action. Just as with question 1, each time this occurs you lose server processor resources and network bandwidth.

3. **Does the program require a swap file on the server?**

This question also is directly related to the issue of program segments and overlays. Some programs try to maintain a unitary vision of themselves. Once an overlay is called in, the program is taught to think that it has "grown" and now requires more RAM than it did before. If the program grows beyond the amount of RAM available, the swapping issue takes over.

Swapping is used to move a section of the computer's RAM to auxiliary storage (hopefully a local hard drive but all too often the user's personal storage space on the server) in order to free up RAM for programs, portions of programs, or data. It's used extensively by multitasking operating systems like Windows and OS/2 to manage memory. Speaking of which,

4. **Is it likely that users will run this program at the same time other programs are running in a multitasking environment like Windows?**

The more stuff the user puts into the environment, the higher the likelihood that the environment will overflow. Running more than one program at a time is a virtual guarantee that swapping will be put into play, and the same network resources will be negatively affected.

5. **Does the program use a shared file set on the server?**

Even if you're a good soldier in the network wars and place programs on local hard drives, sometimes that's not enough. In this age of e-mail and groupware many programs are constructed with sharing in mind, even those that you wouldn't ordinarily think of as sharing types, like databases.

The shared files in use might be as simple as a word-processing program's dictionary file that all users can check and add entries to or as complex as a full client/server database implementation. Regardless of the type, each one steals a little bit of your network's soul.

6. **Does the program maintain a "lock file" on the server?**

This is probably the least of all the application's evils. When you bought the program you bought a certain number of licenses to use it. In order to ensure that you don't have more users working with the program than you are legally entitled to, either the program itself or another program will monitor the number of simultaneous users and "lock out" any beyond the legal number.

Lock files are typically very small and have a minimal impact on network performance, but remember, we're talking about the cumulative effect here.

7. **Does the program use a proprietary or "nonnative" communications protocol to communicate with other programs or with other instances of itself?**

Here's a definition for you: *insidious. Webster's New World Dictionary* defines it as "*adj.* 1. characterized by treachery or slyness 2. more dangerous than seems evident." Adding protocols is the very essence of insidiousness.

Some programs decide that for their own reasons the network communications protocol you use isn't good enough for them. A communications program might decide that instead of Novell's native IPX/SPX it wants to use TCP/IP or, God help you, NetBEUI. Every time you add another protocol to the network you're taking a huge bite out of the bandwidth available to you. In some cases the amount taken is completely out of proportion to the benefit gained.

Here's an example: If your network has a UNIX minicomputer with Portable NetWare, you're probably using Novell's NetWare Virtual Terminal (NVT) protocol to talk to it. I'll bet you didn't know that NVT takes every single keystroke that the user types and turns it and it alone into a network packet.

Depending on the type of network you use, that single keystroke just became a packet of 64 characters (Ethernet), 124 characters (Token Ring), or 508 characters (ARCnet) What? You say that they hardly ever type a single character alone? Too bad, my friend. The more they type, the more gummed up your network is getting.

Each of these questions you answered in the affirmative took away anywhere from a little bit to a huge gaping chunk of your network's overall capacity. In many cases there isn't anything you can do about it, other than to be aware of it and plan for upgrades and speed increases whenever and wherever practical.

If you're really concerned about where your network is and how much more stress and strain it can take, you'll want to look into obtaining a network traffic analyzer, either as a permanent acquisition or by renting, borrowing or stealing one. No, scratch the stealing part. You're probably in enough trouble already.

Network Traffic Analyzers

Network traffic analyzers, also called protocol analyzers, are devices that attach to the network cable to watch, interpret, and diagnose problems that might occur (see Figure 6.2). They're either standalone hardware devices or combinations of hardware and software, such as a special card you put in a PC along with software for that PC.

Once in place the traffic analyzer watches every packet that passes across the network and can tell you how many of which kind of packet was sent, what the sizes (and contents if you're nosy) of those packets were, and how much of the network's theoretical capacity was taken up. They're really useful for a number of different tasks, and if they weren't so flinkin' expensive everyone would have one.

If you're going to buy a traffic analyzer, plan on spending at least $2,000 for a simple, single-topology model and $5,000 or more for a top-of-the-line unit capable of dealing with high-speed network types (like Fast Ethernet). If you're going to rent one, it'll cost you around $200 for a week, but you'll likely get at least that much money's worth of use out of it.

Figure 6.2   Network General's Sniffer network traffic analyzer. Photo courtesy of Network
             General Corporation.

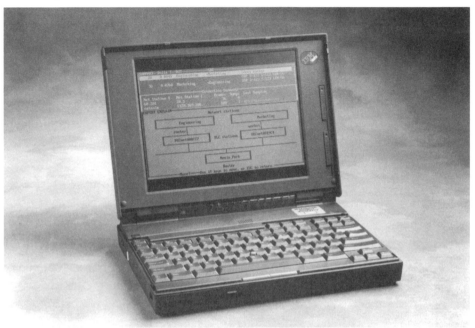

Once you have a traffic analyzer in place it's a perfect time to play around
with your network configuration to see how different applications, datasets,
or physical configurations affect performance. Go ahead, add that application
to the network and see for yourself how it affects response times by comparing
the "before" and "after" information. Try segmenting the network with a
router or by putting multiple network cards in your server to see how much
performance you get back. In short, experiment! It'll be worth it.

HOW FAST SHOULD I DO ALL THIS?

You've probably guessed by now that this isn't a trivial exercise.
Collaborative computing will change the way your company does
business, both internally and externally. Departmental boundaries will be
eroded or eliminated, and the concept of "boss" and "subordinate" will also
come under heavy fire.

We've spilled a lot of ink telling you how to prepare the network, but how do you prepare the people? Going forward with collaborative technologies will require that they give up many of their ideas about how the company works in order to make the company work better.

Lay the Groundwork

The first step to opening the workplace to new ideas is to solicit some of those ideas from your co-workers. Even though you have given significant thought to the whys and wherefores of adding networked multimedia and you now have a pretty good idea of the benefits to be accrued, you have to let most of the people you work with discover them for themselves.

You can't throw all of the concepts and technologies at them at once. Break down your goals into individual applications or components and then toss them into the ring one by one. The best way to do this is with a brief questionnaire.

The first section of the questionnaire should include a paragraph about the technology itself. Explain that this is a new concept and you're wondering (heh, heh) whether it would be applicable to the way your company does business. After you've given the preamble explain the technology in simple everyday terms with an absolute minimum of technospeak. If you do have to use technical terms, explain them.

Once you've explained the application itself and where your interest came from, solicit respondents' ideas. Questions like "Do you find this concept interesting?" and "If we had this program what kinds of things would you want to use it for?" are absolutely perfect for soliciting honest responses.

The questionnaire should be circulated as widely as possible within your organization. Remember that collaborative computing is all about breaking down boundaries and levels, so you'll want feedback not just from the bosses but from the folks who fight on the frontlines day in and day out. Here's a sample questionnaire for getting feedback from the organization about using whiteboarding applications.

New Computer Program Survey

A new type of computer program has become available recently called a "whiteboard." While reviewing the documentation for this program, we became interested in whether or not it would be beneficial to the way that our company does business.

Whiteboards:

A whiteboard program is used to enable the screens of two or more computers that are usually in different places to show the same things at the same time. If one person has a chart on his screen, everyone else who's hooked up can see the same chart and even make notes and modifications for all to see.

Whiteboard programs are typically used with telephone calls so that people at multiple sites can have teleconferences with coordinated visual aids. They can also be used to train people on how to use new programs, to solve problems, for brainstorming sessions, and for sales presentations.

Whiteboard programs can be used within a single office, across a computer network, or even across telephone lines from home to office. They can save a lot of time in setting up meetings, traveling to remote locations, and making sure that resources are present when you get there. They can save a lot of money for the same reasons.

We really want your opinion on this concept. Please take a few minutes to look at the description of a whiteboard program and then answer the questions below. Once you've completed it, return this form to Ralph Randolph in room 1234. Thanks for your help!

Your name _____ Your department _____

1. Do you find this kind of program interesting?

   (A) Yes   (B) Sort of   (C) No

2. If someone else were using this program to do something that you wanted to be included in, would you use the program?

   (A) Yes   (B) Only if I had to   (C) No

3. If you had a project in which you needed to involve people at other locations, would you want to use this program to do it?

   (A) Yes   (B) Only if I had to   (C) No

4. If you had this program available to you, what existing projects or parts of your job might you want to use it for?

   _____

   _____

5. If you had this program available to you, would there be any new things that you could do that you couldn't do without it?

   _____

   _____

6. How many times a week do you think you'd use it? _____

7. Would it make your job:

   (A) Easier   (B) Harder   (C) Wouldn't change it

8. If it turns out that we buy this program and you find that you like using it, would it make you: (be honest)

   (A) More productive   (B) Less productive   (C) No effect

9. If it turns out that we buy the program and you find that you don't really care for it, would using it make you: (be honest)

   (A) More productive   (B) Less productive   (C) No effect

10. Can you think of functions that you're *not* responsible for in the business that would benefit from this program?

_____

_____

11. What do you think of this idea in general?

_____

_____

_____

Thanks for your time! Your opinion is important!

That's it. Short and simple is the key. You don't want to make the questionnaire a huge, complicated thing because people will resent the time necessary to fill it out and their resentment will transfer onto the survey form itself. Instead on getting feedback about the program you'll be getting feedback about the form, which is not what you were after.

The responses will likely be as varied as the people answering your questions. There will be technophiles who think that anything new is wonderful, regardless of whether it's useful or not, and technophobes who think that technology is inherently evil and we should all go back to pounding rocks, living in caves, and being mortally afraid of open flames.

It's the people in the middle who will provide the most valuable feedback. These people will give you calm, reasoned, intelligent responses that allow you to gauge the probable success of the project.

If you're thinking of implementing more than one multimedia application, don't circulate multiple surveys at the same time. Instead, collate the responses from the first questionnaire and include those results when you send the second survey around. Wait at least a couple of weeks between rounds, too. If you got the participants all excited over the first concept (either positively or negatively), you don't want that to rub off onto the next or any subsequent inquiries.

Telegraph Your Punches

Assuming that the responses to your inquiry weren't overwhelmingly negative, you're probably ready to move forward with the project but you can't just go out and install the program and components, and sit back waiting for everyone to use them. The setup is as important as the knockout.

The first thing to do is circulate the results of the questionnaire along with your own comments. Don't attribute comments to individuals, regardless of how smart or inane you think they might be. Summarize wherever possible, and if there are written comments that you want to include, do so but don't attribute them to anyone.

Along with the results attach a brief plan of attack for the implementation. Let people know when you expect to install the application, when they can expect to be trained, and the kinds of things that they will be expected to use it for. Stress that these are guidelines, and if they can think of additional uses you'd love to hear about them. It sounds obvious, but try never to shut off the dialog. The best ideas usually come when you're not trying to collect or generate them but rather when people are feeling relaxed and inquisitive.

Stick to Your Word

If you make a commitment to do something, such as training on the application, make the strongest effort possible to hold to that commitment. If something comes up that delays or makes doing it impossible, communicate that fact, and the events that forced you to modify your plans, immediately. Believe it or not, the biggest part of whether this program succeeds or fails doesn't relate to the program itself but rather to your own credibility.

Once the program is in place, occasional updates are a really good idea. Send around a memo or newsletter that talks about how the program is being used, how people feel about it now (solicit comments from selected people, either written or verbal), how much money is being saved by its use, and in what new ways it's being leveraged by the organization.

Give It Time

No matter how well or poorly your first foray into collaborative computing went, allow some time for things to settle before you start adding to the mix. There are a number of really good reasons for this.

Remember the three types of user we discussed when interpreting survey results? The technophiles probably jumped into your new system with both feet and started using it for everything regardless of whether or not the use was appropriate. They need time to settle down.

The technophobes are still staring tremulously at that menu option, waiting for it to either dissolve or reach out of the screen and bite them. They need to be brought along gently, and layering more applications on top of their current woes is not the way to do it.

And then there are the folks in the middle. They looked at it, they used it, they looked at it some more, they used it some more, and now they're busy integrating it into their daily work. They've discovered that it's fun and really does make them more productive, so they're thinking about other ways to use it to make life even better. You want to let that process take its natural course.

How long will it take? That depends on the nature of the collaborative technology and how widespread its use is. Even the smallest company or group of users won't get through this process in less than a month. Most large systems will take two or three months to settle out, and cutting-edge technologies may take as long as six. You'll know it's time to move on when the technophiles get bored with it and the technophobes stop calling for basic support.

Ah, the psychology of technology implementation. This is something that's overlooked all too often, with results that range from negligible to disastrous. On the one hand you're bringing new tools and toys to the network that people will enjoy using and that will make their jobs simpler and more productive.

On the other hand, you're introducing change into the environment that some will find alluring and others threatening. You have to accommodate both of those extremes and keep the ones in the middle interested. But you know what? It's worth it.

7 BUILDING A NETWORKED MULTIMEDIA GROWTH PLAN

One thing that we haven't talked about yet is vision. It's obvious that you already have a vision of what you want the finished network to look like, simply because you bought this book. You're looking for ideas and justifications that will allow you to go forward with your vision and bring the benefits of sound, light, and movement to your network.

HOW TO SAY WHERE "THERE" ACTUALLY IS

The fact that you have a vision for the future is neat. But it's not going to do you any good if you can't articulate it, explain the benefits and liabilities of following it, and get the people who hold the purse strings in your organization to sign on for the duration. The best way to do this is by using an innocuously named little piece of paper: the Direction Statement.

THE DIRECTION STATEMENT

Direction Statements allow us to formulate goals and decide on measurable ways of achieving those goals, but those aren't the only things they're good for. Because the Direction Statement contains all of the components of the project, including resources to be consumed, costs, and time frames, it becomes the corporate vehicle that you'll use to drive the project to completion. Your company may have specialized documentation that needs to be completed as well, like capital expenditure authorizations or project summaries, but all of this follows a single clearly defined Direction Statement.

A properly executed Direction Statement is fairly formulaic in its organization, but it should read like good literature rather than a business memo or project summary. It's divided into nine very tight sections:

1. Introduction

2. Project Definition

3. Goals

4. Benefits

5. Costs

6. Components

7. Timeline

8. Success Measurement

9. The Future

Each section should be reasonably short, and the entire document should be less than five pages long. By creating and submitting a Direction Statement for approval, you're creating a roadmap for the project to follow. You'll write the directions for each leg of the journey, in the form of project summaries and implementation schedules, as you go.

The best way to understand the purpose and nature of the Direction Statement is to look at one and then discuss its individual components. Below you'll find a description of a fictitious company, Amalgamated Widgets. After that we'll walk through each section of the Direction Statement.

The text that you would create as Amalgamated's Information Systems manager is shown in italics. A discussion of that text follows each section.

Case Study: Amalgamated Widgets, Inc.

Amalgamated Widgets, Inc., is a medium-sized company. Corporate headquarters is in Salinas, Kansas, where the factory and main distribution center are also located. There are two regional distribution centers, one in San Bernardino, California, and the other in suburban Boston, Massachusetts.

There are also seven sales offices scattered about the country. Each office has its own local area network, and all of the LANs are tied together by a wide area network composed of dedicated 56K leased circuits. Take a look at the map in Figure 7.1 to get a better idea of what the company is all about.

Computer operations at Amalgamated are pretty simple right now. All accounting is done at Corporate HQ except for inventory operations at the two regional distribution centers. The sales offices have all the usual suspects, like word processing for proposals and bids and spreadsheets for sales analysis and forecasting.

The company uses MobyMail, a Windows-based electronic mail system that has all the latest features, but it is currently using it only for traditional text-based mail.

Figure 7.1   Amalgamated Widgets, Inc., corporate map.

As Information Systems manager of Amalgamated, you realize that your company is ripe for networked multimedia. Communication between the various offices is limited to telephone and e-mail right now, and you believe that productivity is suffering and costs are too high because of it. You begin to consider which pieces of the networked multimedia pie are right for your employer.

One of your department's tasks is user training. Because the Sales department has a fairly high turnover, you've had to send a member of your staff to each of the sales offices at least twice a year. It occurs to you that using a whiteboarding application and a speaker telephone would be a good way to perform user training without actually having to be there.

In everyday discussions with co-workers around the company, you notice that a common theme is that people in the sales offices and at the distribution centers feel cut off from the day-to-day operations and decisions that are made at Corporate. The thought strikes you that providing video-enabled e-mail with recording capability for selected persons at the corporate office and playback-only capability at the remote offices will encourage management to stay in better touch with the rank and file.

You decide to bypass sound-only e-mail for a couple of reasons. The first is that sound-enabled e-mail isn't compressed, and the amount of bandwidth on the wide area links would negatively impact the overall speed of the network. The second is that of the nine locations in the company, six of them already have voice mail, so you'd just be duplicating a capability with only a small cost reduction to show for it.

For the same reason, you eliminate videoconferencing, at least for the time being. Once people get a taste of video-enabled e-mail it's only a matter of time before they want to talk back, and it's usually a *very* short time after that until they want it in real time. You'd better build a growth path to videoconferencing into the Direction Statement.

The Introduction

Introduction

*The Amalgamated Widgets, Inc., Information Systems department has a unique opportunity to provide better, more useful, and more exciting features on our internal computer network while maintaining our excellent reliability and reputation for cost-effectiveness This document provides an overview of the desired applications and technologies, along with cost-effectiveness studies and timelines for implementation. Each section is summarized below, with the section name in **boldface**.*

Grab them! Notice how this section gives a tantalizing glimpse of what you're up to without giving anything at all away. You're using words with a strong positive semantic content, like "better," "excellent," and "cost-effective."

As short as it is (typically only a single paragraph) you want to achieve two specific goals with this section: to establish that you're talking about a sexy new computer tool or tools, and that they'll have to read further into the document to find out what you're proposing. This creates in the reader a sense of curiosity and also sets up some inertia. Even if they get the gist of what you're talking about in the next few paragraphs they'll continue reading just to see if you have any more surprises up your sleeve.

At this point you're ready to construct a Project Definition.

The Project Definition

Project Definition:

We can be at the forefront of networked computing by applying multimedia technologies to our existing wide area network to offer new applications that make users more productive and more satisfied with their jobs, and that provide significant cost savings to the business.

We currently use a wide area network for company-wide communications and user support. The network is designed to support text-based communications such as electronic mail and the transportation of documents from location to location.

*Because the network is limited to text we are missing several excellent opportunities. Shared application viewing, commonly called whiteboarding, can be used for collaborative work on design and problem-solving projects, and can also be used by Information Systems to provide better and more cost-effective training. There are other **Goals** that Information Systems hopes to achieve with this project.*

*Adding the ability to record and transfer video electronic mail from the corporate office to our field locations will enhance company communications at every level and result in widespread improved productivity. These and other **Benefits** are discussed in this document.*

*If approved, this project not only will be cost-effective but will return significant cost savings to the business that can be used to improve operating results or to fund additional projects. Complete information on expected Return On Investment (ROI) is provided in the **Costs** section.*

*This document also details the **Components** that Information Systems intends to add to the network, the benefits and costs associated with these additions, and the **Timeline** to complete this project. **Success Measurements** are also cited at the end of the report to assist management in assessing the success of the project.*

*In **The Future**, we may choose to implement other technologies that build on the systems included in this document. For example, video electronic mail is included, but videoconferencing is not. If we were to add this technology now major changes would be required to the structure of the network, and there would be large costs associated with the changes.*

Once whiteboarding and video e-mail have been in place for some time, employees will become more accustomed to collaborative computing. We can re-evaluate real-time technologies such as videoconferencing at that time and make a cost-based decision.

This section is critical to the success of the project. In the "Introduction" you grabbed readers by both ears and said, "Listen up!" This section tells them the specifics of what you want to do. If it's not exciting and visionary, you may well lose your audience, and it's unlikely that they'll give the rest any more than a cursory once-over, if you even get that much.

So what exactly is it that we're trying to accomplish here? The Project Definition is both your vision statement and a road map. It should state in general terms where your organization is now, where you want to get it to, and how you plan to get it there. Don't go into detail because that's what the rest of the document is all about.

You should expect that not every reader is going to read every single word, because different people will have markedly different interests in what you're trying to tell them. Sales and Marketing may only read the "Goals" and "Benefits" sections to figure out what's in it for them. Finance may only read the "Costs" section to find out what the expense is, and "Human Resources" may very well zero in on the "Success Measurements" section. That's okay. If you have something for everyone, then everyone's going to read something.

Be as upbeat as you can in this section. If you're using conditional words like "should," "could," and "might," take them out. Be truthful, but speak only in absolutes. Leave the conditional items for the rest of the document, where you can expand on them at length and explain the variables involved.

The format is an easy one. Start with where you are by summarizing the systems that are currently in place. Try to begin at a neutral position and gradually get more enthusiastic as you talk about the exciting possibilities for the future. Don't start by "talking down" the existing network. After all, you built it, and you're supposed to be proud of it. What you're aiming for is an "Aw shucks, it's okay, I guess" kind of attitude.

Once you've established the current position, tell readers what components you want to add to the environment and what good those components will bring, in one or two sentences per application at the most. You'll go into further detail in the "Goals" section, so tell them so.

Next, use one paragraph to summarize the positive changes this will bring to the business and refer them to the "Benefits" section for the rest of the story.

After that it's time for the words that bring joy to the hearts of accountants everywhere. Tell them you're going to do all this and save money in the bargain. Did you notice in the sample that it says the savings "could be used to fund additional projects"? That should earn you a belly laugh from top management, but look at it this way: If you don't ask, you don't get.

You can lump together references to the "Components," "Timeline," and "Success Measurements" sections in a single paragraph. By this time either you've hooked them or you haven't, and only people who are sincerely interested and who expect to be affected by this project will be heading for those sections.

Remember to include technologies that fall outside the scope of the current plan, but that are being taken into consideration for future growth, in a section called "The Future" or something like that. This is, after all, a vision statement, so be prepared to be visionary.

The Goals

Multimedia Project Goals:

The first networked multimedia application to be added to our network will be a whiteboarding application. Whiteboarding will allow groups of people around the company to work together at the same time on documents such as sales proposals and contracts. It will also allow Information Systems to conduct user training on computer applications without having to travel to the individual sites to do so.

After whiteboarding has been fully implemented we will add the ability for selected individuals at the corporate office to create and distribute electronic mail that contains the digital equivalent of videotape, and we will give users at all sites the ability to play back these video clips on their individual computers from within their e-mail programs.

In this section you're listing all of the technologies you're going to add to the network and the tasks that people will use each technology for.

Use a broad brushstroke here, like "video-enabled e-mail" rather than list the camera, sound board, and other assorted pieces of whatnot. You'll do that in the "Components" section, and, frankly, most people will skip that part. After all, it's up to you to make all the blinky boxes work. *How* they work is of very limited interest to most people.

Notice that in this section we're not going to talk about the "why" of doing these things. We're reserving that for the "Benefits" section, and, again, we're doing it to maintain that sense of curiosity and keep the reader digging further into the document. We will scratch that curiosity bump in the very next section because you can only carry this technique so far. If you do it too much, the reader will become irritated, and irritated readers don't continue reading.

If it sounds to you like we're setting up the plot for a mystery novel, you're not too far off the mark. Make this a dry, dull technical document, and only dry, dull technical people will read it—that's not your intended audience.

Make it intelligent, bold, and exciting, and you'll be thought of as intelligent, bold, and exciting by extension. Just don't show them this book.

No, wait. Maybe it would do them some good to be bold and exciting too. Buy them a copy of this book for their own use. No, buy two copies, one for home and one for the office. Oh, and maybe one to read on the train home. And one for the kids, and one for the dog, and they make great Christmas presents and . . . sorry. Got carried away for a second.

The Benefits

Benefits to Amalgamated Widgets and Its Employees:

It is expected that we will realize many benefits from implementing these technologies. These benefits will range from direct cost savings on day to day operations and measurable productivity improvements in many groups to intangible benefits such as improved job satisfaction and better company morale through improved communications. Each application has specific benefits to the organization:

Whiteboarding

The whiteboarding application will allow groups to work together from disparate sites without incurring the cost and time of travel. According to Sales and Marketing, there are, on average, three meetings each quarter of the Sales organization to coordinate sales proposals. These meetings are often held at hotels near the sales office coordinating the bid, and costs per meeting, including travel, lodging, and food, are approximately $10,000 per meeting. The whiteboarding application will eliminate these costs. Additionally, each person attending the meeting typically spends one full day of traveling to and from the meeting, with a concomitant reduction in productivity. Since personnel will no longer have to travel from their home site, productivity will be enhanced.

Information Systems sends one trainer to each site quarterly to perform new user training and give refresher courses. The trainer stays at the site for two to five days each trip. Again, travel time incurs a one-day productivity penalty. With the whiteboarding application, training frequency can be increased, multiple sites can receive training simultaneously, and the travel expense is eliminated entirely.

Since the whiteboarding application has such broad appeal, it is expected that other groups will also take advantage of this technology in new and unexpected ways. For example, Manufacturing may choose to conference with Distribution to collaboratively develop more accurate sales forecasting spreadsheets.

Video-Enabled Electronic Mail

A common complaint across the organization is that the remote sites feel all too remote from day-to-day operations of the rest of the organization. Becuse of cost and time constraints, upper-level managers do not travel to the sales offices as often as is desirable, and consequently people in field offices feel a little (or more than a little) left out of the mainstream of events. The company newsletter helps to alleviate this, but it deals mainly with larger issues, and because of production constraints, the only things that are communicated are events that have already occurred, sometimes with a significant time lapse between the event and its reporting.

Video-enabled electronic mail will allow management to present a timely, humanized face to the organization. Simple text-based e-mail is good in that it allows the communication of information quickly and efficiently, but it lacks the human touch. Tone of voice, facial expression, and body language all combine to deliver a "message within a message" that is lacking in standard e-mail.

Video e-mail eliminates many of these liabilities. Anyone with the requisite equipment attached to his or her computer can quickly and easily create and distribute messages of virtually any length to individuals, groups, sites, or the entire organization. For example, assume that a salesperson in the Chicago office receives an award for exceeding quota this quarter. If the Chairman sends a text e-mail congratulating her, it gives some measure of satisfaction, but the employee might wonder whether the Chairman actually sent the e-mail or whether his secretary simply called up a standard document and sent it off under his name.

If the Chairman takes two minutes (literally) to record a video e-mail directly congratulating the employee for her performance, there can be no doubt. That employee knows that her efforts have been noted and applauded at the highest level of the company. She will in all probability show off the message to her co-workers as well. Others will realize that outstanding performance really does get noticed and will redouble their efforts on the company's behalf.

The benefits of using video-enabled e-mail are subtle, and probably more powerful than we realize by virtue of that subtlety. Measurement of improvements in productivity will be more difficult to obtain, but there are methods, such as user surveys. Please refer to the "Success Measurements" section below for additional information.

You must have noticed that this section is quite a bit longer than the sections that preceded it and quite a bit more specific as well. We've used up the curiosity gambit, and, as promised, we're going to scratch that bump for them as completely as possible.

In this section you should break out the individual technologies you're proposing. Explain each one as it relates to how the company does business now and how that will change with the implementation of this technology. Use specific examples wherever possible that illustrate with word pictures how much better the lives of people who are affected by this application will be.

Continue to wax effusive about the many wonderful things that you will be bringing to the organization by implementing these technologies. Don't be shy or modest here. Because the technologies are so new, both to the computer industry and to the way that most companies do business, you really need to hit the high notes and make management understand that your plan represents a major improvement in the way things are going to get done. Be positive and upbeat here to the point that people will accuse you of terminal optimism, but stick to the truth. It won't be hard. These really are wonderful, beneficial new technologies.

You should be as specific as possible about the benefits that you have identified, but be sure to add a sentence or two about how even you can't forecast all the ways in which this stuff is going to be used.

That's true, by the way. No matter how well we think we understand the business, we really only understand a small part of it, so involve those people who do the rest of the things in your company in the process. The odds are very good that they'll come up with ways to use your new toys that are cost-effective, productivity-enhancing, and that you never would have thought of in a million years.

When you write this and the following sections, divide them into the various applications that you are proposing for the project. Try to maintain the same order as you go through the document so that readers can follow your logic more readily.

The Costs

Cost/Savings/Benefit Analysis:

Costs of this project will be quite reasonable, especially when compared against expected savings. As is shown in the "Return on Investment" section below, full cost recovery occurs very quickly when direct costs alone are taken into account. When expected productivity increases are added, the return of capital is very quick indeed.

Whiteboarding

The whiteboarding application can be implemented immediately and has no additional hardware requirements. Adding this capability to the network requires only that we estimate the number of concurrent users at any given time, purchase the requisite number of licenses, and install the program.

We will assume that up to twenty computers may use the whiteboarding software in a single session. This may include more than one person per computer, but the cost analysis is based on one person per computer.

Savings are based on the elimination of three sales conferences per quarter at $10,000 per conference, and the elimination of five out of nine Information Systems training trips per quarter at $1,500 per trip. The reason that all nine are not eliminated is that we often combine training visits with general maintenance and repair of network equipment. Some actual travel will still be necessary.

Software Cost:	*$4,000*
Savings (one quarter):	
Sales and Marketing:	*$30,000*
Information Systems:	*$7,500*
Net Savings:	*$33,500*

The return on investment is actually less than one month, and implementing this technology will save the company $146,000 in the first year of operation. These savings can be partially applied to the next application, "video-enabled electronic mail," and will show an overall rate of return that is extremely rapid.

As you will see below, video-enabled electronic mail returns enough benefits to the company to justify approval on its own merits.

Video-Enabled Electronic Mail

The basic assumption is that upper management (vice-presidents and above) at the corporate office will receive the equipment that allows the creation of video e-mail (a total of eight stations), and all computers within the organization that are capable, or can be made capable, of viewing video e-mail will be so equipped. As of the most current equipment inventory, 30 stations are "video ready" at this time, 35 will require additional RAM memory, and 20 will require both additional RAM and a faster video display controller. All video-enabled stations will require sound boards and external speakers. There are currently 41 stations that cannot be upgraded cost-effectively to be video capable.

Costs:

Video cameras (8)	*$16,000*
Additional RAM	*$5,000*
VGA accelerator cards	*$2,000*
Sound boards	*$10,000*
Speakers or headphones	*$6,000*
Videoconferencing software	*$8,500*
Total	*$47,500*
Savings*	*$170,000*

*This assumes an overall corporate productivity increase of 2 percent. Based on 1994 payroll information, total gross payroll was $8,500,000, so savings are represented as $170,000.

Return on investment comes at 3½ months, and the first-year net saving to the company is $122,500.

This section actually does double duty. You're going to be giving them a "bad news–good news" type of presentation, where the fact that you'll have to spend money on implementing these goodies is offset by the fact that you'll actually be saving the company money by creating savings opportunities.

Because you'll be buying things to attach to or load onto the network, these things are considered by the accounting people to be "capital improvements" rather than "costs." We'll still call them costs, though, as it means that money will be flowing out of the company, at least initially.

For each item provide an itemized list of costs to as close an estimate as you can achieve. Since this is a preliminary document, if you can get to within about $500 per line item you're doing pretty well. Do not, repeat, *do not*, underestimate costs. If you're unsure as to the actual amount, deliberately overestimate them.

It's really important to balance those costs against the savings and show exactly how long it will take for the company to realize savings that exceed the money laid out. This is called "Return on Investment," or ROI, and it's the yardstick against which virtually all capital improvements are measured. If your project has an ROI that exceeds two years, it's doubtful that you'll get the project approved.

Don't stop at the point that the project has paid for itself. Be sure to calculate how much money the company will save in real dollars during the first year and make that the last item for each application. If you're proposing three or more applications, you should provide a summary with the "bottom-line" savings for implementing all of your proposals as well.

If the project doesn't pay for itself in the first year, don't fret or panic. Simply calculate it based on a two-year payback period. If it doesn't pay back inside the two-year window, it's time to sweat and panic because the likelihood that the project will be approved is vanishingly small. In all probability the only way that you'll get it approved is by proving conclusively that it has other, nonmonetary benefits, like increased competitiveness in the marketplace or public relations value.

After the costs you should provide the potential savings numbers, again as closely as possible. If the numbers aren't self-evident, then you should explain where they came from and how you got them. If you can't be exact, estimate, and do the exact opposite of what you did with cost items by shooting *low*.

Whatever happens, if this project is approved you don't want to be surprised. The worst possible thing that you can do is find out later in the project life cycle that costs were too low or the savings too high (or, in the absolute worst possible case, both were true) and have to go to management with hat in hand and foot in mouth. It's far, far, better to go with a pessimistic estimate and be proved happily wrong. That way you can go to management and say that things are better than you expected and the savings will be even greater. If you're really lucky, you work for a company that provides incentives for cost savings and a portion may find it's way into your pocket.

The Components

Components of the Multimedia Project:

The whiteboarding application has a single component only, the software itself. Video-enabled e-mail has two sets of components, one for the stations capable of both creating and viewing video e-mail and the other for those stations that will only be able to play back messages.

The computers that will be set up as originators of e-mail will all be Intel 80486-class computers with 8 megabytes or more of RAM. These computers are already in place, so no additional chassis will need to be purchased. To the basic computer we add: a Charged Coupled Device (CCD) video camera, a video capture board, an external microphone, a 16-bit sound board, and either speakers or a headset at the user's preference.

Stations to receive video e-mail must be Intel 80486-class running at 33 Mhz or faster. Eight megabytes of RAM are required to achieve full frame rates, as is an accelerated video card or local bus card if the computer is capable of accepting one. Additionally, a sound board and either speakers or a headset will be required.

Information Systems has reviewed a number of manufacturers of video cameras and their associated software. The system selected is XYZ Systems' model 2,000,000 B.C. This system offers the widest range of features at the lowest per-station price.

Manufacturers for the sound boards, speakers, and headsets have not been selected yet. Each of these items approaches the level of a commodity in the marketplace, and it is anticipated that Information Systems will select the lowest-cost "Sound Blaster" compatible sound board.

Here you're filling in the details. As we said before, most people are going to skip this section, but you still need to have it, if for no other reason than that you're proving that you really have thought the whole process through, identified potential suppliers, and verified ballpark costs.

If you know who the manufacturers and/or vendors will be at this point, it is appropriate to put their names into the Direction Statement, even if the information changes as you continue to refine your plans

Be techy. Be nerdy. Be techy-nerdy. In this section it's perfectly all right. Those who read it are going to be one of two types: Either they will understand and be excited by the neat new toys you're going to be deploying, or they're nontechnical types who will simply be reassured by the fact that you appear to know what you're talking about.

Don't try to double-speak or throw in good-sounding gobbledygook. There will be people reading this document at some point who do know what you're talking about, and if they find out that you're trying to snow them, it could be a job security issue for you. In plain English that means you could get fired.

Don't be surprised if management elects to have an independent consultant review this Direction Statement in its entirety. You're likely to be the most, if not the only, technically qualified person at your company, and we *are* talking about a lot of money. If management does this, you should take it as a very good sign. They're serious enough about evaluating your vision to spend money on a second opinion. As long as you're sure of your technology and facts, you'll come out just fine.

The Timeline

Project Timeline:

Because of the low cost of acquisition and immediate savings, Information Systems plans to buy and install the whiteboarding application within the next 30 days. Our own personnel will be trained in its use both as participants and in "train the trainer" sessions during the next month.

After the acquisition, installation, and Information Systems internal training, we will make the application available to other groups within the company. The first group to receive it will be Sales and Marketing. We anticipate that this group will need to conduct a bidding strategy conference within 30 days of receiving access to the whiteboarding application.

Instead of having the conference, Information Systems will lend Sales and Marketing a support tech/whiteboarding trainer who will remain with the participants throughout the "conference."

Once this first live exercise is completed Information Systems will begin training at least two persons from each site in the use of the whiteboarding application as administrator of a multiperson collaborative session. The training process will take less than 30 days. The whiteboarding application will be fully deployed within the organization in under 120 days (four months).

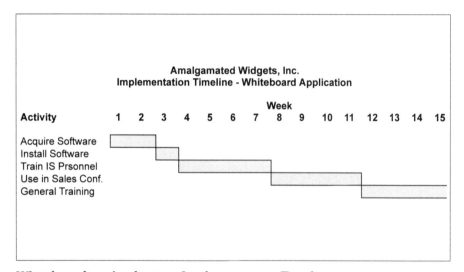

Whiteboarding Application Implementation Timeline

Rolling out video-enabled e-mail will take a longer period of time because of the number of computers involved in the project and the necessity of opening each one to perform upgrades and install additional components.

During our support tech's regular visit to each site, he or she will spend an extra day at the site performing hardware upgrades, new hardware installations, and software installation (the Video for Windows drivers). Because of the number of sites and the infrequency of visits, the complete hardware/software installation process for all sites will take up to 60 days from project approval.

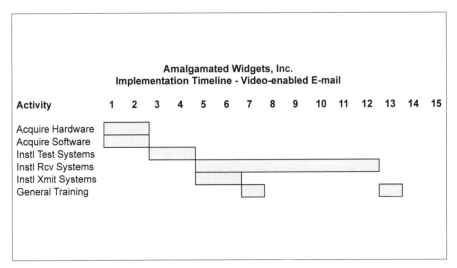

Video-Enabled Electronic Mail Implementation Timeline

Installation of the hardware necessary for video creation will be accomplished simultaneously with upgrades of the receiving workstations. Information Systems will create two "test" installations, which will be transferred to vice-presidents' offices when optimal configurations are achieved.

Training in how to create video e-mail clips will take one day. Two training sessions will be scheduled to accommodate busy executive schedules. Please refer to the project management schedules above for complete information. The "zero point" for both schedules is the date of capital expenditure approval.

In this section we're laying out just how long it's going to take us to provide these goodies to the user community, when we plan on training them in how to take advantage of them, and when we expect the goodies to become a useful part of their day-to-day jobs.

The project management charts aren't completely necessary, but they help a lot. We have to use a fair amount of techno-speak (geek gabble?) in order to describe accurately what's going to be happening. Using charts allows the nontechnically-inclined to look and say, "okay ... first they buy the stuff, then something incomprehensible happens, then something else incomprehensible happens, then they train me, then I get to use it." And for most of them that's really all they need to know.

The Success Measurement

Success Measurement:

There will be two major methods of success measurement employed for this project. the first method is a simple balancing of costs against direct cost savings. Information Systems will obtain cost data from Accounting, and a cost/savings report will be produced at 90 days, 180 days, and at the one-year mark. As was described earlier in this document, we anticipate that all of the direct costs will be offset by direct savings within the first six months after these new systems are fully implemented.

The second method will be by user survey in order to measure levels of job satisfaction (and by extension productivity). The surveys will be "blind;" in other words they will not *be administered by Information Systems. The first survey will be taken before there is any mention of these new applications to the user population and will form the baseline of employee job satisfaction for measurement against subsequent surveys.*

It is anticipated that Human Resources will be interested in the results of this and subsequent surveys for its own purposes. Information Systems will coordinate with Human Resources to develop the survey form so that both groups can take as much benefit as we can.

A second survey form will be sent out six months after full implementation of the new systems. This survey will be identical to the first (although in keeping with good user survey practice, the questions will be moved around on the form even though the questions themselves remain identical). Three months after that an additional survey that deals specifically with the whiteboarding and video e-mail applications will be sent out for user response.

The desired result is twofold: First, a rise in user job satisfaction of at least a mean of 5 percent. Second, positive user response about the new applications as a result of the third survey.

It should be noted that we are looking for a 5-percent increase in job satisfaction rating but applying only a 2-percent productivity increase. The higher number is intended to offset any other positive external changes in the user's workplace. If there are any negative changes in the workplace, such as realignments or restructuring (not anticipated but always possible), it will be very difficult to provide a quantifiable measurement. This is a common sociometric hazard and is, unfortunately, unavoidable.

As for the people who are going to make the decisions about whether or not to approve the project, this is the do or die section. It's all very well to talk about how your vision will make life wonderful for everyone around you, but at some point along the line you have to provide a way to test what you say will happen against what actually happens.

In certain circumstances this can be really easy. Take the direct costs for example. One way to find out if your project is a success is to determine whether or not it saves the company money. If you're getting the same job (or more jobs) done on less cash, you're a success. If you're not, you're in trouble. In most cases how much trouble depends on how much cash you ended up costing the company.

The indirect costs or savings can be trickier. Measuring productivity increases or decreases can be done in a fairly straightforward manner, but you can never be really *sure* that you got back numbers that are valid. What if business was very slow at the beginning of the measurement period, but picked up steadily and was unusually brisk at the end of the period? Your results would look like a huge productivity gain, but they would be only marginally related to your efforts.

Job satisfaction is another item that can be measured but will either gain of suffer from external events. There are sociometric analysis methods that take these sorts of things into account, but describing them goes about a million miles outside the scope of this book.

Realistically, the only thing you can do here is hedge your predictions by noting that stuff you can't control could knock the whole thing into a cocked hat. You should be a little more businesslike about it, but that's the gist of the message you want to convey.

Notice the reference to Human Resources in the center of this section. If you remember the last chapter, where we talked about how receptive the Human Resources staff would be to almost any networked multimedia application, you'll see why we're bringing them into the fold now.

Be sure to talk to them about this project *before* you commit them, even on paper, to a heavier workload. Enlist their assistance by showing them the Project Definition before submitting it to management, and get their approval and support up front. We're trying to win friends and influence people, not make enemies and antagonize them.

The Future

The Future:

The concept of networked multimedia is a very broad one, and there are many technologies that Amalgamated Widgets could conceivably benefit from that are not being proposed in this document. Some of these technologies are still emerging and the associated costs are too high; others require too much change, either in the network infrastructure or in the way we do business.

The items not proposed are evolutionary components of a modern network. As Amalgamated's people become more comfortable with new technologies and new ways of conducting business, we will re-evaluate them. Some may be more cost-effective than at previous evaluations and others may fit more closely with the structure of our networks at a later date.

Examples of networked multimedia applications not being proposed now include multimedia presentation graphics software, groupware, sound-only-enabled electronic mail, and videoconferencing.

We have also not addressed the potential benefits of global connectivity via the Internet, or extending the benefits of our multimedia network to our customers and vendors. However, these are all worthwhile goals, and we will certainly examine them more closely at a later date.

For now we have selected technologies that can be implemented quickly with a minimum of disruption to operations and a minimum of training, for maximum benefit to the business.

Since this is the Definition Statement for implementing multimedia on your network, it will be referred to many times during its life for guidance, for resolving points of contention and for looking to the "next step." It follows that the "next step" should be present in the document.

You need to clearly indicate the scope of the technology and the components that are within the scope but outside the project. It is really important that you clearly explain just why those items fall outside the scope and whether you expect that to change in the future. If you miss this step, it will be perceived as arbitrary or, worse, readers will think you left them out because you thought they would be too hard to do.

With that in mind remember that this section does serve to reinforce your expertise with those who will approve the project. What you're saying here is, in essence, "I know a lot of stuff, and some of the stuff I'm not going to tell you right now because you don't really need to know and here's why you don't need to know it."

On occasion someone's going to come back to you and tell you that they do need to know some of the things you left out. If you're going to get questions about the Definition Statement, they're likely to come from two areas. Some people may question how you arrived at your savings estimates or may question the assumptions that you used to derive those numbers. Others may see items in this section that intrigue them, and you may be asked to expound on them a bit, so be prepared to do so.

This can be a good thing. It may be that you have underestimated the need or interest in a component that was not selected and you'll need to rethink the Direction Statement to include that item. Perhaps someone in another department sees cost-effective uses for a technology that you were unaware of or hadn't considered, so be prepared to rethink, revise, and resubmit. It happens quite lot in the "real world."

SUMMARY

The Direction Statement is a very powerful vehicle for developing a vision of how you want to get your network from a bland, text-only here to an all-talking, all-singing, all-dancing there. Once the vision is developed all that remains is to sell it to the people who write the checks, and the Direction Statement comes in really handy here as well.

If you take your time and do it right, selling the concept to management should be an easy thing. It's a matter of where you put the effort because you should be able to tell by now that actually creating the Direction Statement and doing the supporting research are not that easy.

You'll have to study the technologies thoroughly. This book is the starting point, but there are many other sources of information, including manufacturers, resellers and, magazines on the outside, and people, costs, and attitudes on the inside.

A successful Direction Statement requires not only a clear idea of what you want to do but a good understanding of why you want to do it and who you're going to do it to. If these three things are understood and understandable, you stand a pretty fair chance of getting to play with the latest toys.

8 WHERE DO WE GO FROM HERE?

All of the techniques and technologies discussed so far have been either "right here, right now" or "just around the corner" stuff— in other words, things you're likely to want, need, or desire in the immediate future. If we take a look a little farther out in time, the crystal ball gets a bit hazy, but there are some trends developing that will be likely to have an impact on your personal and professional life in the future.

How far in the intermediate future? Oh, a long time — at least two to five years.

TRENDS IN TECHNOLOGY

Nothing ever stands still, least of all technology. It is said (probably by *them*. Who are *they*? I want to meet them.) that the sum total of human knowledge doubles every seven years. Given the events of the past century, including the automobile, air travel, space travel, the computer and 900-number phone sex lines, I hardly doubt it.

This raises three troubling questions. First, where are we going to put all this accumulated knowledge? Second, how are we going to be able to find any single item in that mass of raw data? And last, how much of it is actually worth keeping?

Where Are We Going to Put It All?

The answer to the first question is a fairly simple one. We're already seeing the answer put into practical, everyday use: CD-ROM. Optical storage provides large quantities of extremely stable information that is quickly accessible.

Today you can purchase a CD-ROM drive that stores 660 megabytes of information in raw digital format or in audio or video format. The CD-ROM disc will retain that information completely intact for 100 years or more, as long as you don't leave it on the dashboard of your car.

A CD-ROM disc costs less than $2 to produce and can be placed in a $100 device in your $2,000 computer to be read back quickly and accurately at 150 kilobits per second. If you've got up to $500 burning a hole in your pocket, you can buy a CD-ROM drive that will read back twice, four times, or even six times as fast as that.

What about tomorrow? And the day after tomorrow? Toshiba and Sony are in the final stages of hashing out standards for the next generation of CD-ROM storage media and devices. Since the process isn't completed, I can't give you the exact numbers and descriptions, but it looks like these next- generation CDs will store eight gigabytes (8 billion bytes) of data, or up to two hours of high-resolution, full-motion video at 30 frames per second, and they will deliver that information at two megabits per second. These CD2 devices will likely be available in late 1996, and as with so many other technologies, they'll probably show up in the home first as small, fast videodisc players.

There are those who say that CD-ROM is a dying technology and that on-line delivery of information is the next big thing. To that we say "Pfffagh!" The major limitation in on-line delivery is, now and for the foreseeable future, bandwidth. Do you have any idea how long it would take to deliver 660 megabytes of information, even if you could afford LAN-native speeds via technologies like SMDS?

If you had a 10-megabit-per-second link to the information provider, it would still take 8.8 minutes if you were the only user on the channel. Odds are that you wouldn't be the only user, and network congestion would make that number significantly higher. However, for the sake of argument let's say that you did receive the information digitally over a high-speed link. Now where are you going to put it? On a hard disk, of course. And the other 10 or 20 downloads that your users have requested? You're going to have a capacity problem almost instantaneously.

Some proponents of on-line delivery say that's not the way the information will be organized at all. You'll only get the parts you actually need, and you'll pay for it as you get it. This is also problematic, as far as I'm concerned. What if there are multiple people in your organization who need the same information independently? Why should you have to pay for the information each time one of your users wants to access it? CD-ROMs allow you to purchase the data once, have it available all the time in a very inexpensive format, and make it available to all who need it at little or no cost.

In the meantime hard drives will continue to grow in capacity while shrinking in size and getting faster. According to a spokesperson at the hard-drive manufacturer Maxtor, by the year 2000 the average hard drive will store five gigabytes, retrieve data in the average 5-millisecond range, and cost around $500. It will also be two inches across by about three inches deep and less than a half-inch tall in order to be plugged in to desktop and laptop computers and unplugged as required.

Floppies will get smaller, store more information, and be faster as well. IBM engineers and scientists are working on new-generation media that manage to pack almost 80 megabytes onto a 2-inch floppy disk, and Iomega Corporation has recently introduced a 3½-inch, magneto-optical floppy drive that stores 100 megabytes and costs around $200, with the 100-megabyte floppy disks costing around $25. Information is stored and retrieved from these floppies at roughly eight times the speed of standard floppies, or about half the speed of hard drive, and the drives are capable of reading and writing other 3½-inch diskette formats.

How are we going to back up all this data? There are several schools of thought on this. One school says that since hard drives are getting cheaper and smaller, it would be easiest simply to use a removable hard drive that you can plug into a slot on your computer to take backup and then unplug and store until the next time you use it. The enabling technology for this method is already in place with ultra-small hard drives and PCMCIA Type III and IV slots for portables and desktop computers.

The other school maintains that tape storage, probably Digital Audio Tape (DAT) or its successor, will remain a cost-effective way to store large quantities of information. Next-generation DAT tapes and drives will store up to 25 gigabytes on a single tape with data compression, and read and write that information at up to 20 megabytes per second.

How Are We Going to Find What We Need?

This is beginning to be a problem even now. Giant databases are fine things as long as you have some method of finding the needle in the haystack, whether you use a metal detector or just roll around until you feel a sharp pain.

But databases are really constructed for homogenous data. The more types of data you have, the less a database is suited for them. A few word processing documents, a spreadsheet or two, and some graphics image files all thrown together make a nice collection of information but a really lousy database.

There are two approaches to locating data in large, heterogeneous data sets. The first is to use a hierarchical list server—sort of a directory of directories that allows you to categorize your information and then "drill down" from the top of the directory until you find what you need. If you think of the Internet's World Wide Web as a giant, distributed data set, then trying to making sense of it all by constructing a list of lists really does work. Most people nowadays try to locate information on the Web by starting at Yahoo (http://www.yahoo.com), a "list server" that contains over 200,000 entries in 20 basic categories and thousands of subcategories.

The second approach is a much more radical one. Since it takes human beings a fairly large amount of time to search through documents trying to locate references that they need, why not set the computer itself to the task? "Intelligent Agents" are special programs designed to do just that. They can examine thousands of documents per second while looking for the reference you sent them after, and then report back with the results.

These intelligent agents are autonomous programs. You tell them what you want and then set them loose on the computer, on the network, or on the world. When they have finished their task, they come home to roost and tell you the results. This autonomous design is actually a lot like how computer viruses work, and, in fact, these programs are sometimes referred to as benevolent viruses, which doesn't help their image one bit.

Still, this looks to be the most efficient way to manage the problem of organizing massive amounts of data, because if you have too much data you simply throw another agent at the problem. Instead of launching one agent, you can launch two, three, or dozens and have them all go their separate ways and compare results when they're done.

This brings us to the next major trend in technology. Programs continue to grow in size and complexity. Newer ones may not be a single program at all but a collaboration of processes that talk to each other through programming tools called "threads" or "pipes." In five years your desktop PC may look like it's running a simple application as far as you're concerned, but behind the scenes it may be running several dozen child processes even as several of your neighbors send intelligent agents through looking for documents (assuming you gave them permission, of course).

In order to handle that growth of complexity processors have to get faster and have lots and lots of RAM. Intel's Pentium processor was almost 50 percent faster than its predecessor, the 486, and the P6 is reputed to be capable of being twice as fast again. Projections say that by the year 2000 the typical desktop PC will run as fast as a 1985 Cray supercomputer did, but take up a hundredth of the space and a thousandth of the cost. PCs will also have 64 to 256 megabytes of RAM (which will come on a total of three chips).

So we'll have incredible amounts of information, fantastic ways of organizing that information, and magnificent computers on which to create, modify, and retrieve the information. But what about the data itself?

How Much of This Is Actually Worth Keeping?

Okay, so we have a prodigious amount of information. What guarantee do we have that the information we have spent so much time collecting and organizing actually has any value?

There *are* no guarantees, of course, but the bare fact of the matter is that it's all going to have some value to someone, somewhere, sometime. Here's an example.

In the late 1960s builders in Philadelphia had to halt a major construction project when they accidentally discovered Benjamin Franklin's cesspit. What value could a 200-year-old cesspit possibly have? It turns out that even the lowest (no pun intended) of artifacts has tremendous value to the right person.

In the 1700s it was common to use the cesspit as a trash bin as well. Break some pottery? Down the hole with it. Bend up that old serving fork? Toss it in the pit. A cesspit of that era is a treasure trove of colonial artifacts, but it's not just the household items that have informational value.

Even the stuff they originally dug the hole for has valid data. By analyzing the coprolites (fossilized you-know-what), modern researchers can tell what people of that age ate, how much of it they ate, and how healthy they were overall.

Without being too base about it, it just goes to show that if you wait long enough, even old offal will have some value to someone. The same principles also apply to data. What we consider dated, outmoded, and valueless will doubtless be a priceless find to some researcher a few years down the road.

Enough generalities. Let's take a look at some specific technologies that will change how we think of networked multimedia and even how we'll define it in a couple of years or so.

THE AGE OF VIDEO

Sesame Street. Mr. Rogers' Neighborhood. Barney. The Six O'clock News. We all grew up watching the television set, and we as a society are becoming accustomed to having information delivered in a visual format. Because of this societal trend, we tend to regard information delivered via video as preferable to mere textual information.

An excellent example of this is the new CNN at Work program. A special version of CNN's *Headline News* is distributed digitally via your cable provider and arrives at a special converter box attached to the network. Individual users run a Windows-based program to "tune in" to the news right on their computer screens whenever they want. Rather than calling up to the AP or UPI news feeds and reading the news, users have the news delivered to them visually, with a professional announcer who sorts and disseminates the information in "real time."

This service has both advantages and disadvantages. Looking at the advantages first, we see that the information is delivered in a timely fashion and is preformatted for easy mental consumption. It's easy (comparatively speaking) to get access to the data, and as long as the programming at CNN retains its usual excellence, the data is meaningful and relevant.

On the down side there is no selectivity. In other words, you don't get to search for news that interests you alone and you have to watch it all to get the parts you need. There's no way to record the news you want to keep in a compact fashion (it can be stored, but only as full-motion video, the way it arrived), and it requires some action on your part to activate the recording mechanism to keep the parts you want to retain.

Even so, for all its shortcomings this is a harbinger of the future. The day is fast approaching when we'll be able to do all of the things that we can't right now with regard to distributed video.

Video on Demand

The big boys are playing in this backyard. Cable TV systems have a tremendous amount of bandwidth capacity that's not being used, and they plan to put it in play with interactive video and video on demand. The old lament of "500 channels and nothing good to watch" won't be operative a few years from now.

By storing video digitally, either on huge hard-drive arrays or on quick-access CD-ROM jukeboxes, cable providers will allow you to use your remote control to order movies, TV programs, classes, or any other stored video information, and have it delivered where and when you want it. Oracle Corporation is in the process of creating a version of its namesake database specifically designed to manage and distribute video for cable companies, and other companies are working on the hardware aspect of delivering so much information so quickly.

As with other technologies, it's only a matter of time (and not much time at that) before this one gets smaller, simpler, and cheaper, and moves into the office. In the next ten years expect to find servers for the local area network that allow users to search for the kinds of information they need; that deliver that information whenever they want it; and that store it, organize it, and make sense of it for them.

Your users will be able to pick they way they want to experience that information as well. Just the middle fifteen minutes? No problem. Audio track only? You got it. A transcript in word-processing format? On its way. As with any other tool for the network, all it will take to implement is blood, sweat, and money.

Switched Video Networks

Without meaning to sound too futuristic about it, the day will come when making a phone call is an old-fashioned thing that we only do when we have to talk to people in the jungles of the Amazon or other isolated portions of the world.

Even though AT&T has been trying to convince us for years that videophones are right around the corner, they really haven't been. Bandwidth was, is, and always will be the problem. Until a few years ago the very best data transfer rate you could hope for across the phone lines was 57,600 bits per second, and that was under ideal circumstances. Static line noise, distance, and atmospheric conditions all conspired to keep the practical maximum well below that on a regular basis.

This level of throughput is way too low to support video phone calls. Early videophones were really just jokes, and even the "telephones of tomorrow" that were demonstrated at Disneyland a few years back were techie tricks designed to look like regular phones that really weren't.

That's changing now. Two technologies are developing that may very well mean real, honest-to-God video on the desktop in the very near future. One works with your telephone lines, and the other with your network. They're likely to be competitive with each other, which means that you'll have a choice of methods and that prices are likely to start low and stay that way.

INFORMATION DELIVERY METHODS

The way that you receive information, both business and personal, on a daily basis is likely to be quite different just a few years from now. The concept of private networks will be considered quite quaint, and almost everyone will subscribe to one of several public data networks.

If your company needs a private network, you'll still be using the public one but you'll sign up for a private *virtual* network and be charged accordingly. Just whose public network it's going to be on is up for grabs.

How the Phone Company Sees the Future

The first method uses phone lines. What we think of as a telephone line has changed over the years, but in ways that have been largely hidden from us. In the old days a phone line started at the wall of your home or office as a pair of copper wires, continued out to the street where it hooked to another pair of copper wires, ran for a few miles into the telephone company's Central Office where it was switched onto another pair of copper wires, and so on, until it arrived at a pair of copper wires attached to the wall at your calling destination.

The wires in your home or office may still be copper, but that's about all that's left anymore. They now run down the street to a brand-new telco switch that's compatible with Signaling System 7, and the blasted thing uses fiber optic cables to communicate with all the other SS7 switches scattered all over the country (and soon the world). These switches can handle data rates in the gigabit range (actually 2.1 gigabits per second), and increasing capacity simply means laying another hair-thin fiber optic cable right next to the first one.

The Integrated Services Digital Network (ISDN) that we discussed earlier is a key feature of leveraging that huge network capacity to bring video to the home or office. By applying ISDN technology to the little bit of copper that's left in the system, we can increase the capacity of your home phone lines from the old standard of 57,600 bits per second using audible technology, to 1.544 megabits per second using digital technology, or ISDN Primary Rate Interface (PRI), all the way into the home. If we layer compression on top of that, you can see that this is more than enough to provide full-color, full-motion video across the phone lines and leave room for one old-fashioned phone call or ten.

You can actually have this technology right now if you're willing to pay the $1000 or so for installation, the $5000 for hardware, and the $800 a month for service ("You pay *how much* for your phone service???"), but there isn't anything you can really do with it right now other than make 24 high-quality phone calls simultaneously. Just wait a couple of years, though. The price of service will drop precipitously along with the cost of the hardware and software to make it all happen.

Home videophones probably won't look like the telephones of today with a TV screen tacked on. In fact, it'll probably be the other way around. If you buy into the phone company's vision of the future, you'll likely hook up your TV set to the phone network of tomorrow, and phone calls, movies, TV programs, and all the other *accoutrements* of modern life will arrive via the television.

There's one other way to do this. It's (you should excuse the expression) godawful expensive, but the telephone companies have very deep pockets and smell lots of money if they can become the providers of all your information and entertainment needs.

In my neighborhood there have been a lot of AT&T trucks around lately. I didn't really pay much attention to them other than to note that they appeared to be laying big, high-bandwidth, multimode fiber cable along a route that I travel to and from work. I figured that they were just improving an existing circuit or establishing a new backbone for long-distance service through the area, which is something that the telephone companies do around here all the time. It was a pain to drive through the neighborhood because of the construction, but it was interesting to watch progress on the work. After all, you don't see fiber backbones being laid every day.

My neighborhood is sandwiched between two large industrial areas with lots of commerce and high-tech companies in both areas. The businesses located here use a lot of telephone and data services, so it seemed logical that AT&T was simply increasing capacity to meet their needs.

It wasn't until I noticed that there was a fiber terminator in every single front yard along the route that I put two and two together. AT&T was wiring for multi-megabit voice, video, and data right to the doorstep of every house in this neighborhood! The cables being placed are actually capable of carrying over 2 billion bits of data per second at current technology levels, and there are preliminary reports that, by changing the equipment at the ends of the cable but not the cable itself, over 10 gigabits per second are possible.

They are spending millions upon millions of dollars to make this the most technologically advanced community in America. I was awed. I was also depressed because I live just outside the area actually being wired and I want it. I want it bad.

Late Update! They called me! AT&T called me! They *are* adding fiber to my neighborhood and called to schedule a time to dig up my driveway for the new cable run. I told them that any time they want to dig I want to watch and I might even help them dig if it means I can get 10 megabits-per-second Internet access any sooner.

How the Cable Company Sees the Future

If you listen to your cable company, you'll have a similar view of things to come, but the phone company won't be part of it.

Even though the bulk of the cable "network" is coaxial rather than fiber optic, it still has a tremendous amount of untapped capacity. The cable that runs down your street making its friendly entry into each house along the way can transport around 500 megabits of data per second. Cable companies are busy adding two things to the network that will be necessary to support the applications of tomorrow: switching and interactivity.

Switching is necessary because right now the network can only support 500 megabits per second end to end. This is insufficient for providing video on demand to the millions of households in typical markets, so in order to support the populace efficiently, cable companies are doing the same thing that network managers are doing: segmenting the network. Once that's done each segment can handle that 500 Mbps, and the network capacity jumps by orders of magnitude when segmenting is added.

Interactivity is another matter. Cable systems weren't designed with two-way communications in mind. In order for you to have a conversation with someone, the systems have to know where you are. On the phone network this "where you are" means a unique identifier, in this case your telephone number. Cable companies have to start from scratch with addressing schemes that will allow people to find each other on the same cable system and eventually across multiple cable systems. The equipment in your home or office has to change from simple receivers and decoders to sophisticated transmitter/receiver/encoder/decoder combinations that allow you to receive video, order video when you want it, and communicate by voice and video with other people on the networks. It's a multibillion dollar project, and Time-Warner, TCI, and other cable conglomerates are actively engaged in constructing the networks of the future right now.

We need to consider one more factor. If we're going to have two different standards for video on demand, two different ways of getting it, and two different methods of providing it, how are we going to translate from one to the other? For example, let's suppose that you are on the telephone company's network in Los Angeles and the person you want to "call" is on the cable system's network in Nashville. How are you going to make the jump from one system to the other? Where is this jump going to occur, and who's going to provide the translation and switching equipment to make that jump?

Unfortunately, this is one problem that none of the companies involved seems to be working on actively yet, and this may delay the introduction of these exciting technologies into the marketplace.

However, the day will come all too soon when you'll call Aunt Mabel in Buffalo and not only will you get to hear all about her gallbladder surgery, if you're really lucky she'll show you the scar, too.

INFORMATION SUPERHIGHWAYS

You've certainly noticed that there's a lot of competition out there for your long-distance voice traffic. RealRewards, Calling Oblongs, and other promotional items too numerous to make fun of are all vying for your attention and your dollars.

The same companies that bring you voice traffic also want to bring your data along for the ride, and they're getting pretty aggressive about it. More and more are moving out into the global economy, and as the cost of hardware for turning LANs into WANs decreases, so does the cost of transport services.

Packet-switched networks have really whetted the telephone carriers' appetite for data. Not too long ago, if you wanted a reasonably high-quality line from San Diego to Phoenix, you had to lease a 56K circuit or higher. In essence, you purchased a set of two wires 360 miles long, and as long as you were using them, no one else could. X.25, Frame Relay, and ATM have changed all that.

Now the telcos can sell you a port onto their network and your data can travel the same wires as a whole lot of other customers' at the same time. It really does work out well for everyone. You only pay for your actual data traffic, the telco gets to sell the wire capacity several times over, and everyone's reasonably happy. You still think you're being overcharged, they still want to charge more and push more traffic onto the network, but on the whole it works.

Now add the recent explosion of interest in (and traffic on) the Internet, and things really get interesting. The number of resources on the Net is staggering, and the number of trivial, time-wasting, yet strangely intriguing items is incredible. Add to this the fact that most of the hottest items move, ring bells, or come in 16.7 million colors, and you can see that wide-area public networking is the hottest segment of the multimedia revolution.

THE MULTIMEDIA INTERNET

In the early days of the Internet everything was text-based. The Net itself was composed of a huge constellation of almost exclusively UNIX-based minicomputers. People "on" the Net used character-based dumb terminals, and the hottest tools, like Gopher and Wide Area Information Search (WAIS) were text-based too.

Personal computers changed all that. If you move from a graphical, intuitive user interface, like the Macintosh operating system or Windows, to a textual, UNIX-based interface, you're likely to be considering suicide before too many sessions have passed. There was a very strong need to provide information over the Internet in graphical fashion, and the innovators responded. The result was the World Wide Web.

The Web is a subset of the Internet. Everyone who uses the Internet has access to the Web, but not all computers on the Internet are Web servers. The *lingua franca* of the Web is the HyperText Markup Language (HTML), sometimes called HotMetal in honor of the type foundries that used to turn out slugs used on mechanical printing presses. HTML is a subset of the Standardized General Markup Language (SGML) used for publishing applications on mainframe computers.

HTML allows a designer to select some basic font information and font attributes, such as boldface, underlining, blinking, and the like. Custom backgrounds can also be included, along with simple formatting items like horizontal lines of various widths and colors.

Additionally, you can include graphics in either .GIF or .JPG format and place them in the document, and the result is called an inline image. Common HTML reader programs, called browsers, pull the information across the Net and format it on your PC; the result looks a lot like a printed page of information, which is exactly what the designers intended.

Moving images in .MPG or Apple's QuickTime format can also be included. When a browser encounters these formats, it launches a player program that shows you the movie and then goes back to sleep. Audio alone can also be provided, typically in Apple's .AU or Microsoft's .WAV format. Again, if you select these items, a player program is launched that sings, crys, or rings bells, and then goes back to sleep.

The real magic of HTML is HyperText. Every resource available on the Internet gets a unique address, called a Universal Resource Location (URL). HyperText documents get the prefix "http:," files that can be downloaded get "ftp:," and so on. A typical URL might look like "http://www.green-field.com/pub/index.html," which translates to "the HyperText document located on the Word Wide Web server at the company called Greenfield in the directory called pub with the title index.html."

What makes this cool is that HyperText documents can reference the URLs of other HyperText documents located on the same server or on different servers half the world away. If the link looks interesting, you simply click on it with the mouse and a few seconds or minutes later (depending on the speed of your Internet link) you see the document that was referenced. You can go on like this forever, jumping from document to document, server to server, until your thirst for knowledge is slaked.

Organizations with Web servers and HTML pages accessible across the Net are called Content Providers. They're really publishers, but only in electronic format. At last count there were over 200,000 Content Providers on the Internet, not including the perhaps 1 million users who have personal Home Pages that say a little something about themselves or their hobbies.

That's where things stand right now, but not for long. How would you like to see real-time three-dimensional models on your cruise through the Web? Let's say you drop into a virtual Toad Hall, where you can enter each of the rooms and actually see the perspective changing as you meander through. How are they going to do it? Say hello to the Virtual Reality Modeling Language, or VRML.

Older-style browsers are really just text-formatting programs with some added capabilities, especially the ability to follow links to other documents on other servers. The new generation of browsers goes as far beyond that as a Ferrari goes beyond the Model T.

VRML browsers are actually graphics-rendering engines. the VRML document at the server is a string of ASCII text that describes the object to be modeled rather than actually holding the model itself. As text flows across the Internet to your computer, the VRML engine reads it, interprets it, and builds the model on your display screen. This keeps the amount of information to be pushed across the wires to a minimum and provides the best speed available for processing and display where it belongs—on the local side of the link.

Look for VRML Web sites to start popping up in early 1996, and for these types of sites to be the rule rather than the exception within a year after that.

USING THE INTERNET TO MAKE PHONE CALLS

"Hello, Brisbane? This is New York Calling! For Free!" One thing that most people don't understand yet is that the Internet, at least in its current configuration, is essentially free of cost. Commercial services like Compu-Serve, Prodigy, and America Online all charge for usage in one form or another. The Net is accounted for differently.

You pay for access to the Net, but once you're on it there are very few things that cost any money to use. If you are at a major university or a forward-thinking company, you have full-time Net access for either a fixed fee or no fee at all. As an individual you can get dial-up Internet access from a commercial provider, usually at a fixed price for either unlimited hours or a large number of hours per month, with additional blocks of hours available at very low prices.

So what do you do once you've gotten Net access from your computer? Most people simply go Websurfing, but there's a lot more available than that. How does making free phone calls, to anyone else in the world who has Internet access and the same software that you have, sound? Incredible? Yep, it is that, but it's also true.

There are two companies that sell programs for your personal computer which allow you to make voice phone calls across the Internet to anyone else who has your software. The quality is not up to telephone system standards, but it is quite good, and the price is certainly right: free, free, free.

These programs (InterPhone for Apple computers, Internet Phone for IBMs and compatibles with Windows) both feature full-duplex communications; in other words, both parties on the line can talk and listen simultaneously. You can run the programs over any-speed Internet link from a 14,400-bits-per-second modem connection to full T1 or better access, and it sounds the same.

The programs sell for as little as $59, and the only additional costs associated with them would be for hardware if you don't already have the requisite pieces. InterPhone needs your Mac to have a microphone, and Internet Phone requires a microphone and any Windows-supported sound board. If the sound board doesn't support full-duplex recording and playback, you don't get full-duplex phone calls; if it does, you do, too. That's it.

You would think that these programs would have the long-distance phone companies worried, and they do. In fact, a third shareware product, Internet Voice Chat, which was recently purchased by an unnamed telephone company and withdrawn from service. Whether the telco that bought it will offer it under some new program or just bury it as a threat to its revenue streams remains to be seen.

VIDEOCONFERENCING ON THE INTERNET

Would you be interested in real-time videoconferencing across the Internet? Would you be interested if I told you that you can get reasonable quality at data link speeds as low as 28,800 bits per second over dial-up lines? Would you be interested if I told you that the hardware to do this can be obtained at your local computer store for less than $400 per station? Would you be interested if I told you that the software that controls all this and allows real, live honest-to-goodness videoconferencing is free? I kind of think that you would, so I'd better tell you about it.

The product is called CU-SeeMe. It was developed at Cornell University specifically to allow real-time videoconferencing across the Internet. There are versions for Microsoft Windows and the Apple Macintosh, and it works with another program called Reflector for Sun, Hewlett-Packard, and Data General UNIX-based minicomputers.

Once installed the software allows conversations with up to eight other people simultaneously, but you have to have a dedicated T1 access line to achieve this rate. If you're using a modem to the Internet, only a single conversation is possible—adding more conversations degrades the quality of video too much. If you are on a dedicated 56K link (either ADN or ISDN single B channel), you can usually get two or three conversations simultaneously, but no more.

Hardware requirements are minimal. CU-SeeMe doesn't require a Coder/ Decoder board (CODEC) or any other fancy hardware. All you need is a video capture board like the Video Spigot (now called the Sound Blaster SE100) from Creative Labs, Inc.; a low-resolution black-and-white CCD camera (The Connectix QuickCam is commonly available at less than $100); a sound board; a microphone; and speakers.

You don't need a fancy color camera with pan, tilt, zoom, and automatic coffeemaker, because CU-SeeMe can't use them. Black-and-white is all that's supported, and in order to keep the bandwidth low it only supports 4-bit greyscale (which means 16 shades of grey), making for some pretty contrasty images.

That's one of the two major limitations of this technology. The other limitation, also due to bandwidth, is the size of the window in which CU-SeeMe images are displayed: The big windows are 320 × 240 pixels; if the image gets too jumpy, you have to switch to the small windows, which are only 160 by 120.

For multipoint videoconferencing you have to connect to the other participants through a Reflector site. There are quite a few of these on the Internet, and they're all public, so they don't charge you for the connections. You can set up your own Reflector site, but you'll need a UNIX minicomputer to do it on, drastically increasing the cost of the system.

If you're only going to do point-to-point videoconferencing with CU-SeeMe, you can do it on your own LAN as long as you support the TCP/IP protocol. Since you'll be routing images over the local area network at Ethernet or better speeds, quality is likely to be quite good even with the "big" windows.

Cornell University has signed an agreement with White Pine Software for the latter to maintain and enhance CU-SeeMe. According to the terms of the agreement there will always be a "basic" free version of the software available, but White Pine will produce (for sale, naturally) an "enhanced" version that supports all sorts of things, including color over higher-speed connections, phone book management, and security.

WHERE CAN I FIND MORE INFORMATION?

If you have Internet access, there are several list servers that have excellent information available. The best is probably the Yahoo directory of directories. Einet Galaxy is also excellent, and if you're searching for a particular item of interest, don't forget to use the Lycos search engine at Carnegie-Mellon University. If you don't have Internet access, get it. No excuses.

Below you'll find a very small portion of the topic headings available on Yahoo alone. The items listed change daily and the topics change every so often, too, so check Yahoo yourself. The Universal Resource Locator (URL) is http://www.yahoo.com.

There are hundreds of other entries in Yahoo that apply to networked multimedia, but space precludes putting a complete list here. Go play! Have Fun!

Computers:
    Communication
    Documentation and Publications
    Graphics
    Hardware
    Internet
    Languages
    Multimedia (**Important!**)
        CD-ROM
        Companies
        CU-SeeMe
        Distributed Multimedia
        Hypermedia
        News
        Products
        Programming
        Software
        Video
        Videoconferencing
        Virtual Reality

Networks and Data Communication
Software
Telecommunications
World Wide Web

Summary

There's an old Chinese curse that says, very simply, "May you live in interesting times." The next few years are likely to be interesting indeed. Many of the technologies that we've discussed as being currently available but too expensive for most of us aren't going to stay that way for any length of time. There are too many people who would be interested enough to plunk down their cash, if the cash required for plunking was just a bit less. CODEC boards, for example, are likely to plummet from their current $2,000 level down to the $1,000 level and below.

Other technologies are racing forward in popularity, propelled largely by the unanticipated and explosive growth of the Internet. Everyone seems to want to climb aboard this bandwagon, and the number of individuals, organizations, and companies getting "on the Net" is staggering. If you want proof, take a look at the Vendor Guide in Appendix A and see all the World Wide Web sites referenced. That's not an accident. Many computer products and software companies are quickly coming to the realization that the Net is where their customers are, and if they want to keep them happy and attract new ones, that's where they need to be, too.

The future promises to be very colorful, very loud, and very, ummmm . . . moving. See you in it!

Networked Multimedia Vendor Guide

This Appendix is divided into sections and subsections. To find references to the products or services you are looking for, find the main sections for Hardware, Services, or Software; then look for the subsection, such as "Networking Equipment." This is not intended to be a complete reference to every vendor of networked multimedia, but to be a representative sample.

These days there are so many companies getting into the act that a complete reference would require two things: (1) a forklift to get it out of the bookstore and (2) maxing the credit limit on your VISA card.

The following list references the major manufacturers discussed in this book as well as a number of the significant or interesting vendors.

Lawyer talk: "Inclusion of a manufacturer or product should not be construed as a recommendation or endorsement of any kind."

Author talk: "Void where taxed or prohibited by law." "Employees of AP Professional and other sentient humanoids not eligible to win." "Your mileage may vary." "Offer Limited To Stock on Hand—no Rainchecks Please."

Please accept this humble offering in the spirit in which it is offered.

HARDWARE

CD-ROM

Procom Technology

Procom Technology manufactures a line of dedicated CD-ROM servers for local area networks.

Web:	http://www.procom.com
E-mail:	info@procom.com
Phone:	(800)800-8600
Fax:	(714)261-7380
Address:	2181 Dupont Dr., Irvine, CA 92715

Reed Technology and Information Services, Inc.

Reed publishes a line of computer software that allows workstations and general-purpose servers to become CD-ROM servers across a network.

Web:	Not given
E-Mail:	Helpdesk@ocs.com
Phone:	(800)922-9204
Fax:	(301)428-3700
Address:	20251 Century Blvd., Germantown, MD 20874

Processors

Intel Corporation

Intel Corporation is the world's largest manufacturer of microprocessors for personal computers. It also manufactures networking products for Ethernet and Token Ring and videoconferencing products.

Web: http://www.intel.com
E-mail: info@intel.com
Phone: (800)538-3373
Fax: (800)525-3019 (Automated FaxBack service)
Address: 2200 Mission College Blvd., Santa Clara, CA 95052-8119

Motorola Corporation

Motorola is the manufacturer of the 68000 series of processors used in Apple Macintoshes and the PowerPC processor used in Apple Power Macs and IBM PowerPCs. It also manufactures cellular telephones, pagers, and satellite communications equipment.

Web: http://www.motorola.com
E-mail: info@motorola.com
Phone: (708)576-5000
Fax: Not given
Address: 1303 East Algonquin Road, Schaumburg, IL 60196

Networking

3Com Corporation

3Com manufactures Ethernet, Token Ring, and FastEthernet networking equipment, from network adapters for all types of small computer to internetworking devices such as hubs, bridges, and routers.

Web: http://www3Com.com
E-mail: info@3Ccom.com
Phone: (408)764-5000
Fax: (408)764-6740
Address: 5400 Bayfront Plaza/PO Box 58145, Santa Clara, CA 95052

Advanced Computer Communications (ACC)

ACC manufactures the Yukon ISDN router and other wide area networking products.

Web:	http://www.acc.com
E-mail:	info@acc.com
Phone:	(800)444-7854
Fax:	(805)685-4465
Address:	340 Storke Road, Santa Barbara, CA 93117

Adtran

Adtran manufactures a complete line of CSU/DSU interfaces for 56K and T1 applications, as well as ISDN modems and terminators.

Web:	http://www.adtran.com
E-Mail:	info@adtran.com
Phone:	(800)971-8090
Fax:	(205)971-8699
Address:	901 Explorer Blvd., Huntsville, AL 35806

Ascend Communications

Ascend manufactures a line of routers for local area, wide area, and ISDN networks.

Web:	http://www.ascend.com
E-Mail:	info@ascend.com
Phone:	(510)769-6001
Fax:	(510)814-2300
Address:	1275 Harbor Bay Pkwy., Alameda, CA 94502

Hewlett-Packard Corporation

Hewlett-Packard manufactures minicomputers, microcomputers, laptop computers, storage devices, and networking equipment. It is the lead vendor in the 100BaseVG-AnyLAN Alliance.

Web: http://www.hp.com
E-Mail: webmaster@hp.com
Phone: (415)857-1501
Fax: Not given
Address: 3000 Hanover St., Palo Alto, CA 94304

Intel Corporation

See listing under Hardware: Processors.

Network General Corporation

Network General manufactures a line of network analysis products, including various models of the Sniffer network analysis tool.

Web: http://www.ngc.com
E-mail: info@ngc.com
Phone: (800)395-3151
Fax: Not given
Address: 4200 Bohannon Dr., Menlo Park, CA 94025

Storage

Micropolis Corporation

Micropolis manufactures hard drives and high-capacity RAID array systems.

Web: http://www.micropolis.com
E-mail: info@micropolis.com
Phone: (800)395-3748
Fax: Not given
Address: 21211 Nordhoff St., Chatsworth, CA 91311

Sound Boards

Advanced Gravis Computer Technology

Advanced Gravis manufactures sound boards for IBM and compatible personal computers, including the Gravis UltraSound Max full-duplex sound board.

Web: Not given
E-Mail: AdvGravis@aol.com
Phone: (800)324-4084
Fax: (604)431-5155
Address: 1790 Midway Lane, Bellingham, WA 98226

Adlib Multimedia, Inc.

Adlib Multimedia manufactures a number of sound boards for IBM and compatible personal computers, including the ASB 16 Audio System full-duplex sound board.

Web: Not given
E-Mail: Not given
Phone: Not given
Fax: (418)522-4919
Address: 580 Grande-Alle, est, suite 40, Quebec, Canada, G1R 2K2

Spectrum Signal Processing, Inc.

Spectrum Signal manufactures a number of sound boards for IBM and compatible personal computers, including the Spectrum OfficeF/X full-duplex sound board.

Web: http://www.spectrumsignal.bc.ca
E-Mail: info@spectrumsignal.bc.ca
Phone: (604)421-5422
Fax: (604)421-1764
Address: 8525 Baxter Place, Burnaby, B.C. V5A 4V7

Creative Labs, Inc.

Creative Labs manufactures the Sound Blaster family of sound boards for IBM and compatible PCs. It also manufactures the Video Spigot for Windows under license from SuperMac Technology.

Web: http://www.creaf.com
E-mail: info@creaf.com
Phone: (800)998-1000
Fax: (408)428-6628
Address: 1901 McCarthy Blvd., Milpitas, CA 95035

Systems

IBM Corporation

IBM Corporation is the largest computer company in the world. It makes *everything*, including personal computers for home, office, and home/office use.

Web: http://www.ibm.com
E-mail: askibm@info.ibm.com
Phone: (800)426-3333
Fax: Not given
Address: Old Orchard Rd., Armonk, NY

Packard Bell

Packard Bell manufactures home and home/office personal computers that are oriented toward multimedia applications.

Web: http://www.packardbell.com
E-mail: support@packardbell.com
Phone: (800)733-5858
Fax: Not given
Address: One Packard Bell Way, Sacramento, CA 95828

Video Capture

Creative Labs, Inc.
See listing under Hardware: Sound Boards

Video Coders/Decoders (CODECS)

Optibase, Inc.
Optibase is a manufacturer of high-quality, low-cost MPEG encoder/decoder boards for personal computers.

Web:	http://www.optibase.com
E-mail:	mpeg.quality@optibase.com
Phone:	(214)774-3800
Fax:	(214)239-1273
Address:	5000 Quorum Dr., Suite 700, Dallas, TX 75240

Optivision, Inc.
Optivision manufactures MPEG encoder/decoder boards for personal computers and stand-alone devices.

Web:	http://www.optivision.com
E-mail:	info@optivision.com
Phone:	(800)562-8934
Fax:	Not given
Address:	1480 Drew Ave., Suite 130, Davis, CA 95616

Videoconferencing

Target Technologies (C-Phone)

Target Technologies manufactures a wide line of point-to-point and multipoint videoconferencing systems for IBM and compatible personal computers.

Web: Not given
E-Mail: Not given
Phone: (910)395-6100
Fax: (910)395-6108
Address: 6714 Netherlans Dr., Wilmington, NC 28405

Intel Corporation

See listing under Hardware: Processors

Incite Corporation

Incite manufactures a suite of hardware and software for running isochronous Ethernet applications, including real-time video at 16 megabits per second.

Web: Not given
E-mail: Not given
Phone: (800)946-2483
Fax: (214)447-8205
Address: Liberty Plaza II, 5057 Keller Springs Rd., Dallas TX 75248

PictureTel

PictureTel manufactures stand-alone and PC-based videoconferencing systems and software.

Web: Not given
E-mail: Not given
Phone: (508)762-5000
Fax: (508)762-5245
Address: 222 Rosewood Dr., Danvers, MA 01923

Viewpoint Systems

Viewpoint Systems manufactures low-cost point-to-point and multipoint video-only videoconferencing systems for local area and wide area networks.

Web:	Not given
E-Mail:	Not given
Phone:	(214)243-0634
Fax:	(214)243-0635
Address:	Two Metro Sq., 2665 Villa Creek, Dallas, TX 75234

VideoLabs

VideoLabs manufactures a line of videoconferencing hardware and software for the Microsoft Windows environment on IBM-compatible personal computers.

Web:	Not given
E-Mail:	Not given
Phone:	(612)988-0055
Fax:	(612)988-0066
Address:	10925 Bren Rd. E., Minneapolis, MN 55343

Workstations

Sun Microsystems, Inc.

Sun Microsystems is a manufacturer of high-speed graphical workstations, based on the UNIX operating system, with multimedia capabilities.

Web:	http://www.sun.com
E-mail:	webmaster@sun.com
Phone:	(415)960-1300
Fax:	Not given
Address:	2550 Garcia Ave., Mountain View, CA 94043

Silicon Graphics, Inc.

Silicon Graphics is a manufacturer of high-speed graphical workstations, based on the UNIX operating system, that are specifically designed for multimedia applications and design.

Web: http://www.sgi.com
E-mail: webmaster@sgi.com
Phone: (415)390-3900
Fax: (415)960-0197
Address: 2171 Landings Dr., Mountain View, CA 94043

SERVICES

Data Communications: Long-Distance Services

AT&T, Inc.

AT&T is "the Mother of all phone companies." Incorporated in 1885 as the Bell System, it enjoyed a legal monopoly on telephone service in the United States until 1983, when it was broken up into AT&T the long-distance carrier and the seven regional Bell operating companies, otherwise known as "AT&T and the seven dwarfs." AT&T provides global long-distance voice and data transportation services, as well as the ImagiNation entertainment data network.

Web: http://www.att.com
E-mail: info@att.com
Phone: (212)387-5400
Fax: Not given
Address: 32 Avenue of the Americas, New York, NY 10013

LDDS Worldcom (Wiltel)

LDDS Worldcom is the recent merger of Wiltel and LDDS Metromedia. It provides global long-distance and data communications services.

Web: http://www.wiltel.com
E-mail   info@wiltel.com
Phone: (800)737-0773
Fax: (918)588-5295
Address: P.O. Box MD 15-2, Tulsa, OK 74121

Sprint

Sprint is a global carrier of long-distance voice and data services and operator of the SprintLink Internet connection service.

Web: http://www.sprint.com
E-mail: info@sprint.com
Phone: (800)829-0965
Fax: Not given
Address: P.O. Box 11315, Kansas City, MO 64112

MCI

MCI is a global carrier of long-distance voice and data services and operator of the InternetMCI Internet connection service.

Web: http://www.mci.com
E-mail: info@mci.com
Phone: (202)872-1600
Fax: (202)896-2327
Address: 1801 Pennsylvania Ave. NW, Washington DC 20006

Data Communications: Regional Bell Operating Companies (Regional Telephone Companies)

You'll note that most of the companies listed in this section did not provide contact information. Dealing with the RBOCs can be a frustrating experience as they're still the only way to get local telephone service and they know it.

The attitude is "You're going to have to come to us sooner or later, anyway, so we don't have to make any special efforts for you to get to us." Unfortunately for them this attitude is incorrect. Many of the RBOCs offer data communications services outside their regular service areas in competition with national carriers and other RBOCs. But you'd never know it from their attitude.

The companies that ARE listed were prompt and courteous in their replies to requests for information.

Ameritech

Ameritech provides local telephone service in the Upper Midwest. They also provide data communications, cellular and paging services.

Web: http://www.ameritech.com
E-mail: webmaster@ameritech.com
Phone: (312)750-5000
Fax: (312)207-1601
Address: 30 South Wacker Drive, Chicago, IL 60606

Pacific Telesis

Pacific Telesis is the parent company of Pacific Bell, Airtouch Cellular, Airtouch Paging, and a number of other telecommunications related companies. They provide local phone service in the Southwestern United States.

Web: http://www.PacBell.com
E-mail: info@PacBell.com
Phone: (800)722-2355
Fax: Not given
Address: 130 Kearny Street, San Francisco, CA 94108

US West

US West is the local provider of telephone service in the Pacific Northwest. They also provide data communications, cellular and paging services.

Web:	http://www.uswest.com
E-mail:	webmaster.webmaster@uswest.com
Phone:	(303)793-6000
Fax:	Not given
Address:	7800 E. Orchard Ave., Englewood, CO 80111

Bell Atlantic

Bell Atlantic provides local telephone service in the North Eastern portion of the country, including New England. They also provide data communications, cellular and paging services.

Contact Information was not provided

BellSouth

BellSouth is the local provider of telephone service in the South Eastern portion of the United States. They also provide data communications, cellular and paging services.

Contact Information was not provided

Nynex

US West is the local provider of telephone service in the Mid Atlantic states. They also provide data communications, cellular and paging services.

Contact Information was not provided

Southwestern Bell

Southwestern Bell is the local provider of telephone service in the Texas and neighboring states. They also provide data communications, cellular and paging services.

Contact Information was not provided

SOFTWARE

Communications: Voice

Electric Magic Company

Electric Magic is the publisher of NetPhone, an Internet Voice Chat program for users of Apple Macintosh and PowerPC computers. NetPhone allows two Internet users to converse by voice across the Internet on suitably equipped Apple computers.

Web: http://www.emagic.com/netphone/mainblurb.html
E-mail: netphone-orders@emagic.com
Voice: (800)987-2001 or (415)759-4100
Fax: (415)566-6615
Address: 209 Downey St., San Francisco, CA 94117-4421

Vocaltec, Inc.

Vocaltec publishes Internet Phone, an Internet Voice Chat program for users of IBM and compatible personal computers running the Microsoft Windows operating environment. Internet Phone allows two Internet users to converse by voice across the Internet on suitable equipped personal computers.

Web: http://www.vocaltec.com
E-mail: info@vocaltec.com
Voice: (201)768-9400
Fax: (201)768-8893
Address: 157 Veterans Dr., Northvale, NJ 07647

Groupware

Lotus Development Corp.

Lotus is the publisher of Notes, the leading groupware product for personal computers. It also publishes the 1-2-3 spreadsheet program, the AmiPro word-processing program, the cc:Mail electronic mail program, and a number of others.

Web: http//www.lotus.com
E-mail: info@lotus.com
Phone: (800)828-7086
Fax: Not given
Address: 55 Cambridge Pkwy., Cambridge, MA 02142

Operating Systems

Artisoft, Inc.

Artisoft is the publisher of the Lantastic peer-to-peer network operating system, as well as Lantastic for NetWare and Lantastic for OS/2.

Web: http://www.artisoft.com
E-mail: info@artisoft.com
Phone: (800)233-5564
Fax: (520)670-7101
Address: 2202 N. Forbes Blvd., Tucson, AZ 85745

Banyan Systems, Inc.

Banyan is the publisher of the VINES network operating system, loosely based on UNIX with significant networking enhancements. VINES is typically used on very large networks and is popular in Europe.

Web: http://www.banyan.com
E-mail: info@banyan.com
Voice: (508)898-1000
Fax: (508)898-1755
Address: 120 Flanders Rd., Westboro, MA 01581

Microsoft Corporation

Microsoft publishes Microsoft DOS, the most popular desktop operating system for personal computers; and Windows, Windows for Workgroups, and Windows NT—graphical operating environments for small computers. It also publishes a wide range of microcomputer applications for office and home use.

Web: http://www.microsoft.com
E-mail: info@microsoft.com
Phone: (206)882-8080
Fax: (206)93-MSFAX
Address: One Microsoft Way, Redmond, WA 98052-6399

Novell Corporation

Novell publishes the Novell NetWare operating system for local and wide area networks. It also publishes a number of microcomputer applications for home and office use, including the WordPerfect word-processing program for DOS, Windows, OS/2, and UNIX, and the QuattroPro spreadsheet program for DOS and Windows.

Web: http://www.novell.com
E-mail: info@novell.com
Phone: (801)429-7000
Fax: (801)429-5555
Address: 122 E. 1700 South, Provo, UT 84606

Appendix

B

Networking and Multimedia Glossary

ARCnet

A physical organization for tying multiple computers together physically into a network so that they can share resources. ARCnet is the oldest of network types and has many limitations. An ARCnet network operates at four megabits per second and can have no more than 255 computers attached to it.

Bit

A binary digit. Bits have only two possible values, 1 (on) and 0 (off). Eight bits strung together in a certain order represent a byte.

Bitmap

The digital rendering of a photographic image or document. The document is turned into a matrix of dots called pixels, which have values assigned according to whether or not there is any information at that spot on the page and what sort of information it is.

The original bitmaps only worked with black and white and only registered the presence or absence of black—hence the name "bitmap." Current bitmaps can store color information in various depths, and black and white information can be captured in shades of grey, called "greyscales."

Because the information is captured as a matrix of dots, it is also called a *raster image*. The opposite of a raster image is a vector image, which consists of lines rather than dots (see *Vector Image*).

Byte

One character of information stored in the computer. It could be a letter (*A, B,* etc.), the representation of a number (*1, 2,* etc.), or a special character representing any number of things, including the end of a line or page.

Client/Server

A network that uses a centralized computer as a "server" that provides hard-disk space, application execution, shared print services, communication services, or any combination of these across the network to "clients" that do not have these resources themselves. The opposite of client/server is peer-to-peer (see entry).

Coder/Decoder (CODEC)

A hardware device or software program that accepts video captured from a VCR or camera, compresses it at ratios up to 20:1, and stores it digitally in the MPEG format. The CODEC is also used to decode MPEG files and "play them back."

Compact Disc–Read-Only Memory (CD-ROM)

Based on the same technology used to record digital music on compact discs, CD-ROMs store data instead. The data stored can be information, sound, video, or a combination.

CD-ROM discs store 660 megabytes of information in a standard format known as ISO-9660, or the "High Sierra" format. They are evolving rapidly.

Early drives could read information at 150 kilobytes per second, with average data access times just slightly better than those of floppy drives.

Later drives spun the plastic CD-ROM at twice the speed, effectively doubling the retrieval rate to 300 kilobytes per second, and faster movement across tracks also helped to bring the speed up. These were known as "double-speed" drives. More recently quad-speed (600 kilobytes per second) and six-times-speed drives (900 kilobytes per second, 120-millisecond average access time) have become available.

A new CD-ROM format is in the making, promising to increase capacity to around 3 gigabytes per CD-ROM and making even higher retrieval rates possible.

Complex Instruction Set Computing (CISC)

See *Microprocessor*.

Computer–Telephony Integration (CTI)

A technology for giving local area networks access to telephone switches for the purpose of either gathering information (such as incoming telephone numbers) or controlling them (such as outbound dialing under computer control). See also *Telephony Applications Programming Interface (TAPI)* and *Telephony Services Applications Programming Interface (TSAPI)*.

Electronic Mail (E-mail)

Written communications between two or more persons on a local area network, a wide area network, or a public internetwork. E-mail requires addresses, just like regular mail (called *snail mail* by networking know-it-alls), but the address usually follows the form *somebody@ somplace.organization*. E-mail can carry sound, video, programs, or data along for the ride. See also *Multimedia Internet Mail Extensions (MIME)*.

Enhanced Industry Standard Architecture (EISA)

An expansion bus structure for personal computers. EISA was an improvement over the ISA expansion bus developed for original IBM personal computers, Personal Computer/ATs, and their compatibles.

It allowed expansion adapters to run at up to four times the speed of the original specification, and also allowed expansion cards to perform Direct Memory Transfer (DMA) and to take over the expansion bus itself (becoming a bus master) under certain circumstances.

EISA never became really popular, as it was a very expensive specification that added hundreds of dollars to the cost of a personal computer. It was superseded partially by VL-BUS and mostly by the Peripheral Component Interconnect (PCI) specification.

Ethernet

Also known as IEEE 802.3 (although this is inaccurate—Ethernet shares many of the same characteristics of IEEE 802.3, but they are not exactly the same thing). Ethernet is a method of physically tying multiple computers together into a network so that they can share resources. There are three basic types of Ethernet network:

10Base5—10 megabits per second over coaxial cable (type RG-8, the big thick heavy stuff) at up to 500 meters from end to end of the cable. Each device must attach to the coaxial cable with an electronic device called a transceiver. Because all the computers are arrayed along the cable, this is known as a bus topology network. This version is also commonly called Thicknet.

10Base2—10 megabits per second over coaxial cable (type RG-58, thinner, lighter, and cheaper than Thicknet) at up to 200 meters from end to end of the cable. Transceivers are not used here, but no more than 32 computers can be attached to the cable; this is called a segment. If more computers are needed, then additional segments are added along with devices called repeaters to tie the segments together. 10Base2 is also considered a bus topology network, and this version is commonly called either Thinnet or Cheapernet.

10BaseT—10 megabits per second over telephone-style twisted-pair cable. All computers are attached to their own cable, and the cables come together at devices called hubs at distances up to 100 meters. Because of this organization, 10BaseT is known as a star topology network.

Fast Ethernet

Also called 100BaseT Ethernet. This is an expansion of the original Ethernet specification which allows for data communications at 100 megabits per second, 10 times the speed of original Ethernet. It operates over twisted-pair telephone wire or over fiber optic cable.

Gigabyte

A digital billion bytes. Because the computer operates on the binary numbering system (base 2), a gigabyte is actually 1,073,741,824 bytes.

Groupware

Software for sharing documents, electronic mail, images, and other multimedia components across a network. Groupware uses a centralized server concept to keep storage requirements low. If the network is large enough to need more than one groupware server, information is "replicated" from server to server automatically.

Hub

A device that brings workstations together on a local area network. ARCnet, Ethernet 10BaseT, Fast Ethernet, 100BaseVG-AnyLAN, FDDI/CDDI, and ATM all require hubs, although the actual hub construction is different for each type.

In ARCnet installations the hub is an amplifier of sorts that takes signals in from any port, cleans them up a bit, and resends them on each of the other ports.

In Ethernet networks the hub is actually a multipoint repeater that regenerates the signal entirely and retransmits it. It also prevents multiple stations from sending at the same time and can segment stations that are not transmitting properly off the network, so that they don't cause problems for everyone else.

Fast Ethernet, 100BaseVG-AnyLAN, FDDI/CDDI, and ATM all use switching hubs that actually look at the contents of transmissions in order to route them across the network in the fastest, most efficient manner possible.

HyperText Markup Language (HTML)

The language used to construct documents for display across the Internet's World Wide Web. HTML documents support text, graphics, sound, and, to a limited extent, video. See also *Standardized General Markup Language (SGML)* and *Virtual Reality Modeling Language (VRML)*.

H.320

The European standard for videoconferencing across dial-up ISDN telephone lines. Some American manufacturers have adopted this standard for videoconferencing across local and wide area networks as well.

Indeo

Intel Corporation's proprietary method of compressing video information for transfer and storage. To create Indeo files requires a dedicated coder board (although not the same CODEC used for MPEG), but playback of the files can be done on any PC sufficiently fast to support Intel's Video for Windows player.

Integrated Services Digital Network (ISDN)

A digital telephone network that works alongside the existing analog telephone network. ISDN comes in two flavors: Basic Rate Interface (BRI), which consists of two 56-kilobit-per-second "B" channels and a single 8-kilobit-per-second "D" channel (which no one ever uses); and Primary Rate Interface (PRI), with 24 "B" channels and 1 64-kilobit-per-second "C" channel (which no one ever uses).

ISDN offers very high-quality transmission and reception, and because the entire session is digital, calls can be established in as little as a half-second, including going off hook, dialing, connecting, and establishing the transmission rate. A typical modem call on analog lines can take up to 45 seconds to do the same thing.

Internet

Refers to any two networks that are connected in any way. If you have two local area networks that are bound together, either by a network cable or across a phone line, then you have an internet. This is not to be confused with *the* Internet, below.

The Internet

A giant conglomeration of mainframes, minicomputers, local area networks, and individual personal computers that spans the entire globe. As of the last informal survey there were over 10 million host computers and over 40 million users on the Internet.

The Internet originated as a network of government contractors and agencies that decided to connect to each other to share research results more readily, known as ARPAnet (Advanced Research Projects Administration Network). Over the years many universities and colleges attached themselves to the network; then large corporations (mostly defense contractors) joined the party. When college students who had used the Net started to graduate and wanted to be able to continue to access it, the Internet really took off.

Access methods vary from dial-up connections using modems, to slow direct connections at 1.544 megabits per second or less, up to "backbone" connections capable of moving billions of bits per second. The native communications protocol is the TCP/IP protocol suite.

Internetwork Packet Exchange/Secure Packet Exchange (IPX/SPX)

The native communications protocol suite for Novell NetWare networks. IPX is an "acknowledge" protocol, meaning that each packet sent must be acknowledged by the recipient with an answering packet. The SPX protocol does not require acknowledgment, but its structure makes it less useful than IPX.

Even so, IPX/SPX is a very efficient method of moving information across a network, and Microsoft's Windows 95 Network uses IPX/SPX as the native protocol, replacing NetBIOS/NetBEUI.

Industry Standard Architecture (ISA)

The designation applied to expansion buses of IBM personal computers, Personal Computer/ATs, and their compatibles from other manufacturers. It got this name quite some time after introduction, and in fact only got an official name when competing bus structures were introduced.

ISA is not the original expansion bus type for personal computers (the S-100 bus structure introduced in the early 1970s takes that honor), but it has been the most popular. Even personal computers manufactured today with much more advanced expansion buses still have two or three ISA expansion slots to maintain backward compatibility.

Joint Photographic Expert Group (JPEG)

A standard for compressing, storing, and retrieving photographic and photorealistic images in digital format. JPEG is highly efficient at storing detailed images in small files and achieves its efficiency by using a "lossy" methodology that allows image information to be discarded permanently under certain circumstances.

Kilobyte

A digital thousand bytes. Because the computer operates on the binary numbering system (base 2), a kilobyte is actually 1,024 bytes.

Local Area Network (LAN)

A method of tying together multiple computers in a single building, or in several buildings close together, into a single group that can communicate with each other and share files, printers, and other resources. See also *Wide*

Area Network, ARCnet, Ethernet, Token Ring, Fiber Distributed Data Interface (FDDI), Copper Distributed Data Interface (CDDI), Fast Ethernet, NetWare, Windows NT, Topology, and *Server.*

Media Access Unit (MAU)

A type of hub that is used to tie together individual stations on a Token Ring network. Each workstation on the network needs a "port" to plug into on the MAU. If you need more ports, you add more MAUs and hook them directly to each other.

A MAU is actually an entire Token Ring in a single box. Each time you plug a workstation into a port, what you're really doing is extending the ring out to that station and back again in a single cable. That's why Token Ring is referred to as a "star wired ring" topology.

Megabyte

A digital million bytes. Because the computer operates on the binary numbering system (base 2), a megabyte is actually 1,048,576 bytes.

Megahertz

A number representing the operating speed of the microprocessor. While it's impossible to translate a certain number of megahertz into a standard number of operations per second (different operations take different amounts of time to execute), it's easy to compare two microprocessors against each other. The simple rule is "more is better." The larger the number, the higher the speed of the computer.

Be careful if the number is represented as 2/66 or 4/75, though. This means that the processor operates at a multiple of the system board's speed by a technique called "clock-doubling." A 2/66 processor operates on a 33-megahertz system board by executing two instruction cycles for each clock cycle on the main board. A 4/75 or 4/100 processor is actually clock-*tripled* and operates on a 25-megahertz or 33-megahertz system board, respectively.

Microprocessor

The "brains" of a microcomputer. The microprocessor contains a number of pockets called registers that are used to manipulate data by performing mathematical operations on it.

There are two different schools of thought in microprocessor design. The first school holds that you should instructions in the processor's hardware to deal with every conceivable situation. This philosophy is called Complex Instruction Set Computing, or CISC. Examples of processors using CISC are all the Intel X86 processors, including the 8088/8086, 80286, 80386, 486, Pentium, and the forthcoming P6, and the Motorola 68000-series processors for Apple Macintosh computers.

The second school says that you should put only the simplest, most basic instructions into hardware (around 20 percent of the number of instructions in a typical CISC processor), because the processor will be executing these instructions 80 percent of the time. The remaining instructions are handled by combining a bunch of the simple ones through software design. This is called the 80/20 Rule, and processors that follow it are called Reduced Instruction Set Computing (RISC) processors.

Because RISC chips are a lot simpler than CISC chips, they can run a lot faster. The net result is that RISC processors are around 15 percent faster than CISC chips overall.

Modem (Modulator/Demodulator)

A device that hooks up to a computer's serial port and a telephone line and translates the digital data that comes out of the serial port into analog signals (modulates them) for transmission across the phone line. The modem at the other end translates them back into digital (demodulates them) and passes them through the serial port into the computer at the other end.

Moving Picture Expert Group (MPEG)

A standard for encoding, compressing, and storing moving video with accompanying audio. The MPEG standard is in the public domain, and anyone who wants to create a program that uses it or a "video clip" stored in this format can do so without paying royalties. See also *QuickTime*.

Multimedia

The marriage of sound, video, and information on a computer. Any program that uses more than one of these techniques is considered a multimedia application.

Multimedia Personal Computer II Specification (MPC II)

The current specification for what makes a personal computer multimedia capable. It includes the computer's processor (Intel 80386-SX25 or better), RAM (four megabytes or more), hard drive (28-millisecond or faster response time), CD-ROM drive (double speed, or 300,000-bits-per-second transfer rate), a sound board, and video display capabilities (640×480 pixels by 256 colors, capable of 15 frames per second of video).

Musical Instrument Device Interface (MIDI)

A specification for hooking together musical instruments and computers that can pretend they're musical instruments. The MIDI specification is a very simple one that uses cables with only five connectors to transmit and receive information serially at very low speeds (only 14,000 bits per second). Cables are "daisychained," and each device has at least two MIDI ports, labeled "MIDI In," "MIDI Out," and sometimes "MIDI Through."

The MIDI cable transports information about music rather than the music itself, and leaves the actual sound generation to the instruments. Information can travel on up to 32 "channels" in the cable, so a single MIDI cable can control up to 32 "voices" (the musician's word for each individual music source) simultaneously.

Network Basic Input–Output System/Network BIOS Enhanced User Interface (NetBIOS/NetBEUI)

A very old protocol suite for peer-to-peer local area networks. It was originally developed around 1981 and is a very versatile set of commands and data packages that allows personal computers to communicate on a LAN.

NetBIOS/NetBEUI is a very large, slow protocol suite that is not well suited to multimedia applications. It's the native protocol suite for IBM's PC LAN network, Microsoft's Windows for Workgroups, and several flavors of the Lantastic network operating system.

NetWare

A network operating system from Novell, Inc. NetWare is the most popular network operating system in the world, with approximately 60 percent of all file servers using it. There are two popular versions, 3.12 and 4.10. The former is used mostly on smaller local area networks and wide area networks, and the latter is used mostly on larger regional, national, or international networks.

Network Operating System (NOS)

The operating system that runs on a centralized "server" and allows computers on a local area network to communicate with the server and each other and to share resources on the server or other computers across the LAN.

Nybble

Four bits of information. Four bits make a nybble, and two nybbles (or eight bits) make a byte. It's the truth; I couldn't make this stuff up if I tried.

Object Linking and Embedding (OLE)

A method for encapsulating information from one program inside another program in the Microsoft Windows environment. It's often called "drag and drop" because this is how you embed one object in another. Just click on the first object, drag it over to the second object, and drop it in. The raw data, along with information about the link, is stored, and if the original data is changed, any changes are reflected in the linked document as well.

OLE is the enabling "glue" that allows non-multimedia programs to have multimedia features. An example would be using OLE to "drop" a video clip into an e-mail message.

Peer-to-Peer

A way of organizing the computers on a network so that each computer is equal to each other one in terms of ability to share information and resources with other computers on the network. Peer-to-peer hosts can make all or a portion of their drives available to other users, make their directly attached printers available for remote print jobs, and send and receive electronic mail across the network.

It's up to the network manager to decide whether a computer on a peer-to-peer network will be a "host," or provider of information or resources, or a "client" that simply makes use of other computers' resources when it needs them.

The opposite of peer-to-peer is client/server (see entry).

Peripheral Component Interconnect (PCI)

Intel's specification for a local bus expansion architecture for Pentium and later processors. The PCI bus allows manufacturers to produce expansion cards that access the processor at its native speed, allowing for faster through-put of data in the computer. PCI cards are commonly available for network attachment, fast video, hard-drive controllers, and other purposes.

Picture Element (Pixel)

The smallest unit of measurement on a computer screen or stored image, indicating a single "dot" of color. Computer monitors are rated by their capacity to display the number of pixels across by the number of pixels down by the number of colors that each pixel can be. A typical measurement might be $640 \times 480 \times 256$ (640 pixels across the screen by 480 pixels down the screen by 256 colors per pixel).

Stored images often rate the number of pixels per inch, which can be as high as several thousand. Printed documents are often much more detailed and understandable than displayed images.

Protocol

(also *protocol suite*) An agreed-upon method for packaging information to be sent across a local or wide area network. The physical wires carry information, but the protocol defines exactly how that information is packaged.

QuickTime

A standard for encoding, compressing, and storing moving video with accompanying audio. The QuickTime standard is owned by Apple Computer, and people who want to play back "video clips" stored in this format must purchase a license to do so. As of mid-1995 a license cost $9.95 per computer. See also *MPEG*.

Random Access Memory (RAM)

The electronic chip memory in a computer which stores programs currently being executed and their data.

Reduced Instruction Set Computing (RISC)

See *Microprocessor*.

Scanner

A device that takes documents, photographs, and other images and turns them into digital bitmaps. Scanners use the same technology that fax machines use, but at higher numbers of dots per inch and often in color.

Server

A central device on a network that provides services to other devices on the network. The most common type is called a file server, typically a computer with large-capacity hard drives that can be accessed by any user with appropriate security rights; some files can be accessed by multiple users simultaneously.

Other examples of servers are print servers, which allow multiple users to send output to shared printers on the network; communications servers, which allow users to share modems for inbound and outbound data calls; and fax servers, which allow people to send and receive facsimiles from their desktop computers.

Standard Generalized Markup Language (SGML)

A way of coding documents that might be moved between different, otherwise incompatible, computer systems. The document includes information about typefaces, sizes, and positioning, and graphical information.

SGML is the "big brother" of HyperText Markup Language (HTML), the coding method used to prepare documents for display on the Internet's World Wide Web. Some WWW servers can display both HTML and SGML documents.

Telephony Applications Programming Interface (TAPI)

Microsoft's specification for interfacing telephones to desktop computers using either a special device that hooks up to both the computer's serial port and a telephone or an advanced modem. The TAPI specification requires that each computer requiring telephony–computer integration have this software and one of the two devices.

Telephony Services Applications Programming Interface (TSAPI)

Novell's specification for interfacing NetWare servers to telephone switches using software that runs on both the server and the switch and a serial line connection between the two. Since integration is achieved at the server, any computer attached to the LAN with software that takes advantage of TSAPI is computer–telephony enabled.

Token Ring

A local area networking topology that uses a "star wired ring" physical organization. Token Ring operates at either 4 megabits or 16 megabits per second. Because of its design, Token Ring is a very stable and highly secure network type and, for this reason, is the networking choice of most banks and financial institutions.

A recent development is called "full-duplex" Token Ring. This allows stations to send and receive at the same time, providing up to 32 megabits per second of throughput. Unfortunately, most operating systems and applications cannot take advantage of this feature, at least not yet.

Topology

The physical shape of the network in terms of how computers are hooked to each other across the network cables. There are three basic topology types:

Bus topology networks align all the computers along a single cable. The server or servers can be anywhere along the cable. Ethernet 10Base2 and 10Base5 on coaxial cable are bus topology networks.

Ring topologies arrange the computers around a continuous ring. Again, the server or servers can be anywhere around the ring. Sometimes a second ring accompanies the first, and if a break occurs in the cable the first and second rings are brought together to form a giant C-shaped double ring. Token Ring, FDDI, and CDDI use the ring topology.

Star topologies are arranged with each device on its own cable and a device called a hub or concentrator at the center of the star. 10BaseT Ethernet, Fast Ethernet, 100BaseVG-AnyLAN, and ATM are examples of star networks.

Transmission Control Protocol/Internet Protocol (TCP/IP)

A peer-to-peer suite of 15 protocols for local area and wide area networking. The workhorse of the protocols is Internet Protocol, or IP. TCP/IP is commonly used on networks that need infrequent connections between two specific computers, rather than on networks where a client must be in constant contact with a server.

For this reason, TCP/IP is the protocol suite of choice on *the* Internet, as this gigantic global network was designed specifically for connections that are made and broken as necessary.

TCP/IP is an *unreliable* protocol suite. That means that communication packets are not guaranteed delivery to their destination and it is the responsibility of the sender to make sure that data is delivered properly. This makes the network itself very robust, as each sender assumes responsibility for complete transmissions.

Universal Resource Locator (URL)

A standard way of identifying any resource that can be accessed across the Internet. If the resource is a World Wide Web server or a single document on a server, the URL starts with "http://" and might look like this:

http://www.yahoo.com/Business/Products_and_Services

The resource might be a file that can be downloaded using the File Transfer Package (FTP) protocol. If so, the URL starts with "ftp://" and might look like this:

ftp://ftp.risc.ua.edu/pub/pc/win3/winsock/trmptel20.exe

It could also be an electronic mail address ("mailto://"), a Gopher directory manager ("gopher://"), or a Telnet session to a minicomputer or mainframe ("telnet://user@host").

Vector Graphics

The opposite of bitmap graphics. Vector images are stored as lines and curves rather than as matrices or dots. They are typically used only for line drawings, cartoons and engineering drawings.

Vector images are much better than bitmaps at being scaleable. You can make a vector image smaller or larger simply by expanding or shrinking it, and the image stays proportionally correct without losing quality or resolution.

If you expand a bitmap image the individual pixels get bigger and the image starts to look "blocky." If you compress a bitmap image, some of the pixels will be removed and the image loses resolution.

Videoconferencing

Two people (point-to-point videoconferencing) or more (multipoint videoconferencing) at different physical locations talking to each other while able to see each other on a television set or computer monitor.

Video Graphics Array (VGA) Graphics

The standard for displaying color graphics on IBM and compatible computers. There are actually a number of different resolutions for VGA:

Name	Horizontal Pixels	Vertical Pixels	Colors
"Standard" VGA	640	480	256
Hi-Color VGA	640	480	16,784
True-Color VGA	640	480	32,768
Super VGA	800	600	256
Super VGA (Yes, I know)	1,024	768	256

Virtual Reality Modeling Language (VRML)

A coding method for creating and displaying three-dimensional images across the Internet. The author writes a VRML "script" in a language that looks very similar to English. This script describes the object to be constructed on the recipient's screen.

When requested, the script is transmitted across the network to a user with a VRML "engine" program. That program reads and interprets the script and builds the described object or objects on the screen.

These objects don't have to be static. If you want, you can instruct the viewing engine to "walk" around the object and you'll "see" the back side, providing a truly three-dimensional viewpoint.

Whiteboard

A computer application that allows two or more people to synchronize their computer screens across a network so that everyone can see the same thing at the same time. Anyone can make changes to whatever is on screen, and everyone else sees those changes.

Wide Area Network (WAN)

Any group of local area networks connected together by a medium that is not owned by the owner or operator of the LANs themselves. An example would be two LANs in two different cities connected by a digital link leased from the phone company.

Index